Jihad and Jew-Hatred
Islamism, Nazism and the Roots of 9/11

Matthias Küntzel

Translated by Colin Meade

ꟼTP

Telos Press Publishing
New York, NY

Printed in the United States of America
12 11 10 09 08 07   1 2 3 4 5

Originally published in German as *Djihad und Judenhaß*:
Über den neuen antijüdischen Krieg, 2nd ed., Ça Ira, Freiburg, 2002.
© Matthias Küntzel

ISBN-10: 0-914386-36-0
ISBN-13: 978-0-914386-36-0

Library of Congress Cataloging-in-Publication Data

Küntzel, Matthias.
  [Djihad und Judenhass. English]
  Jihad and Jew-hatred : Islamism, Nazism and the roots of 9/11 / Matthias Küntzel ; translated by Colin Meade.
    p. cm.
  Includes bibliographical references.
  ISBN-13: 978-0-914386-36-0 (hardcover)
  1. Terrorism--Religious aspects--Islam. 2. Antisemitism. 3. National socialism. 4. Arab-Israeli conflict. 5. September 11 Terrorist Attacks, 2001--Causes. I. Title.
  HV6431.K85513 2007
  363.325'11--dc22
                                2007031970

Telos Press Publishing
431 East 12th Street
New York, NY 10009

www.telospress.com

Contents

· · · · · · · · · · ·

FOREWORD

· · · · · · · · · · · ·

Radical Islamists hate Jews. They have made that clear long
before and since Al Qaeda attacked the United States on 9/11.
This clarity was manifest in terrorist attacks aimed at Israeli
civilians, denunciations of the "Zionist-Crusader alliance" and
in the attacks on New York and Washington themselves. They
have proudly proclaimed their radical antisemitism in countless books, essays, fatwas, sermons, manifestos and declarations
reproduced in newspapers, on radio and television and on the
internet. As this torrent of Jew-hatred has continued, it has
become obvious to anyone familiar with the radical antisemitism
of the Nazi regime that none of the declarations of Al-Qaeda or
Hamas, or their predecessors in the Moslem Brotherhood nor
the variations offered by Mahmoud Ahmadinejad and the Iranian government are original contributions to the history of
hatred. Unmistakable echoes of Nazism's violent, paranoid conspiracy theories about the evil nature and vast destructive power
of the Jews have been evident in the ideological tracts and political practice of radical Islam since its crystallization during and
after World War II in Egypt. Yet despite the obviousness of these
lineages and echoes, many of the fine works of scholarship and
government commissions on the subject mention the subject
briefly and in some cases ignore it completely.

   With *Jihad and Jew-Hatred,* Matthias Kuentzel replaces this
avoidance with an "unflinching gaze" at the historical lineages
between Islamism and Nazism. He finds it "astonishing that this
undisguised antisemitism has to date received so little attention
in discussions of the motives for 9/11." With this short, powerful,

passionate and thoughtful book, he offers us a corrective of interest to a general interested audience as well as scholars. This is a work of synthesis and interpretation that explores how and why radical Islam emerged as the most important political and ideological movement in world politics to place hatred of the Jews at the center of its ideology and policy following the defeat of the Nazi regime in 1945. This edition is a revised and expanded version of *Djihad und Judenhass: Über die neuen antijüdischen Krieg* (*Jihad and Jew-Hatred: On the New Anti-Jewish War*) published in Germany in 2002. Despite the considerable literature on the topic in English, *Jihad and Jew-Hatred* should take its place as a distinctive and much needed contribution to public and scholarly debate about these issues.

Kuentzel argues that during and after World War II, the center of global antisemitism shifted from Nazi Germany to the Arab world, above all to the radical Islamist currents in and around the Moslem Brotherhood in Egypt. This shift was not due only to the Israeli-Arab conflict. On the contrary, that conflict was made worse by the ideology and policy of radical Islamists. Kuentzel's work implicitly opens up questions which a Eurocentric focus on Nazism neglects. With the defeat of the Nazi regime on May 8, 1945 and then the revelations of the death camps in the months that followed, Nazism ceased to be a major political and ideological force in postwar Germany and Europe. Yet the convergence of Arab opposition to Jewish emigration and then to the state of Israel with the impact of radical Islam in the Middle East meant that Nazism was not discredited in that part of the world to the same extent. So while Nazism as a major movement or state did not persist, disturbing elements of its views about the Jews *found a positive reception in the different language and cadences of radical Islam* in the Moslem Brotherhood in postwar Cairo in particular. Kuentzel's reconstruction impels us to rethink the issue of continuity and break before and after 1945 and expand our horizons beyond Europe to encompass the trans-national diffusion and impact of Nazism and fascism on the Arab and Islamic world.[1]

Jihad and Jew-Hatred has roots in the post-1945 West German and then German tradition of coming to terms with the crimes of the Nazi regime, above all, the Holocaust. Kuentzel is one of a smaller number of German intellectuals who have thought about the aftereffects of Nazism and the Holocaust both inside and outside Europe. To readers familiar with intellectual, political and scholarly developments in post-Nazi West Germany and then in unified Germany, it will not come as a surprise that it is a German author who, more emphatically than any other since 9/11 places antisemitism as the center of examination of radical Islam. *Jihad and Jew-Hatred* stands in long, albeit often minority, tradition of critical reflection on the Nazi past and examination of the nature of antisemitism, that began in the years of Allied Occupation of Germany after World War II and expanded greatly in the past several decades. Kuentzel's analysis of Islamism pushes the effort to face the Nazi past beyond the conventional confines of the period 1933 to 1945. His work suggests that the familiar twelve-year periodization suffers from a certain eurocentrism. When European historians have rethought the issue of continuity and break before and after 1945, we have done so within the context of European time and space.[2] Though in Europe after 1945, Nazism and radical antisemitism were politically and morally in ruins and discredited, Kuentzel reminds us of the striking respectability hatred of the Jews as Jews acquired among radical Islamists in the decades following the war. One implication for historians of this work, is the need to recast the issue of continuity and break in the history of Nazism to encompass its permutations, influences, diffusion and reception outside Europe and in this case, in the Arab and Islamic world in the postwar decades.

Elsewhere, I have argued that the radical antisemitism of the Nazi regime directed at "the Jewish enemy" was composed of a mixture of continuity with old European and German anti-

Semitic traditions along with a break towards an antisemitism of unprecedented radicalism.[3] Kuentzel draws on scholarship on both sides of the Atlantic to make the case that a similar pattern of continuity and break took place in the Arab and Islamic world during and after World War II. It was then that the radical antisemitism of the Nazi regime found an echo in Egypt in the Moslem Brotherhood and reinforced the extremist interpretations of the Koran articulated by Hassan al-Banna and subsequently by Sayyid Qutb. Just as Nazism produced an antisemitism of unprecedented radicalism compared to its European predecessors, so the Islamists active during the conjuncture of ideas and interests in the Middle East in the 1940s and 1950s produced a strain of antisemitism that surpassed in violence and hatred the anti-Jewish sentiments that had been an element of previous theologically based Islamic attitudes. Both Nazism and radical Islam are incomprehensible outside the respective European and Arab-Islamic contexts. Yet both represented a profound radicalization of past traditions.

Kuentzel focuses on the Moslem Brotherhood in Egypt as the ideological reference point and organizational core of radical Islam. In ideology and organization, it echoed themes of European fascism and Nazism, such the subordination of the individual to the collective, celebration of the leadership principle, hostility to liberal democratic institutions, anti-communism, a reactionary attack on capitalism, and the goal of a state based on *sharia* law. Male supremacy, sexual repression, the celebration of jihad and the glorification of a martyr's death in war with the unbelievers (al-Banna celebrated "the art of death") and hatred of the Jews all created points of commonality with fascism and Nazism. So too did the common enemies, Britain and the Jews. During the 1930s, both in Egypt and Palestine, ideological and personal contacts expanded leading to, among other things, the Muslim Brotherhood's decision to distribute the Arabic translation of Hitler's *Mein Kampf* and the flow of German money and weapons to assist the Grand Mufti of Jerusalem, Amin el-Husseini and the "Arab revolt" of 1936-1939 in Palestine against Jewish immigration.

Kuentzel examines the now well-known support for Nazi Germany by Husseini and his staff in wartime Berlin, a support expressed via short-wave Arabic language broadcasts from Nazi Germany to the Arab world. He reminds us that Husseini successfully urged German officials to block efforts for any escape for European Jews to Palestine. Between 1945 and 1948, Islamism received its "most important boost" when the Allied victors of World War II "considered their good relations with the Arab world more important than countering the ideological concoction of antisemitism, Hitler worship, Holocaust denial and the unbridled desire to destroy Israel, of which the Mufti was the supreme component." As wartime anti-fascism and anti-Nazism gave way to the contrasting priorities of the Cold War, France, with the acceptance of Britain and the United States, allowed Husseini to escape prosecution as a Nazi war criminal and instead to find refuge in Egypt.

As a result, Husseini was able to pursue his "second career" in the Middle East leading when, in cooperation with the Moslem Brotherhood, he led the violent opposition to Jewish immigration and then to the state of Israel in 1948. Kuentzel examines the development of Egyptian Islamism after 1948, offers a valuable discussion of Sayyid Qutb's important anti-Semitic essay of the early 1950s, Our Struggle with the Jews, and explores the tense relationship between the Moslem Brotherhood and the governments of Gamal Abdel Nasser, and later Anwar Sadat and Hosni Mubarak.[3] He analyzes the Islamist revival in Egypt and in the Arab world in general following the defeat by Israel in the Six-Day War of 1967 as well as the emergence of Hamas in the 1980s and Al-Qaeda in the 1990s as well as their connections to the ideological and political conjuncture that emerged during and after World War II in Egypt. He recalls various Islamist declarations to annihilate Israel and the Jews and describes the terrorist deeds that followed from them. Anyone, he writes, who kills with the intention of murdering and maiming as many innocent people as possible "is translating a specific Islamist-fascist world view into action." Kuentzel argues that in word and deed the Islamism of the first decade of the twenty-first century remains marked "to this day" by the connections with Nazism that emerged in the 1930s and 1940s.

In 2007, a broad intellectual public now takes for granted that radical antisemitism was the core of Hitler and Nazism's ideology and policy. This was not the case between 1933 and 1945. Actually, in the first postwar decades in Europe and the United States, only a minority of critical intellectuals, historians and Jewish survivors placed the Jewish question at the center of analysis of the Third Reich. It was not until the 1970s and 1980s that it became central in the mainstream of historical scholarship, and in intellectual and political debate. During the Second World War, the Allies generally kept the Jewish issue on the back burner, in part for fear that intense focus on the fate of the Jews might arouse latent antisemitism in their own societies and thus possibly undermine support for the war effort. After the war, some prominent historians continued to claim that antisemitism was not a driving force of the Nazi regime and that Hitler's statements about the Jews were primarily tactical efforts to obscure supposedly deeper motives. There were always eloquent voices expressing a contrary view, but it took decades before what became known as the Holocaust moved from the periphery to the center of discussion of the Nazi era that it now occupies in major works on the subject.

Oddly, there are some echoes of this reticence in the American and European response to Islamism. The flood of books and articles about the origins of 9/11 includes much discussion of modernity and the cultural revolt against it as well as excellent analyses of the emergence of an extreme, fundamentalist inter-

pretation of the Koran in Egypt and elsewhere in the Arab and
Islamic world. Yet even the comprehensive report of the 9/11
Commission appointed by the United States government man-
ages to discuss Sayyid Qutb's world-view without including a
discussion of the depth and importance of his hatred of the Jews.[5]
This has been the case despite the fact that there is a considerable
and growing scholarship that explores the causal connections and
the impact of Nazism on the emergence of radical Islam. Perhaps
this reluctance has to do with understandable skepticism about
the association of fascism or Nazism with any contemporary set
of events. The inflationary use of the term "fascism" or "Nazi"
has often obscured the differences between totalitarian dictator-
ships and simply conservative political parties in democracies.
The association of Israel with Nazism has been a standard theme
anti-Israeli propaganda. Yet the inflationary or misconceived use
of the terms ought not divert our gaze from historical linkages
and ideological affinities when the evidence is there to confirm
their existence. Historians who otherwise urge us to think about
comparative and trans-national dimensions of history or who
draw attention to the impact of Western colonialism and imperialism on the non-Western world, have yet to devote comparable
effort to the impact of the fascism and Nazism on the Arab and
Islamic world. To be sure, radical Islam is not the same as European fascism or Nazism. Yet Kuentzel makes a compelling case
that the personal contacts and ideological lineages are a matter
of public record, and that they contributed to the emergence of
a kind of radicalism which had not existed before in the Islamic
world. *Jihad and Jew-Hatred* challenges us to carefully examine
both similarities as well as differences between these two key
eruptions of radical antisemitism in modern history.

European intellectual and cultural historians have long
understood that what George Mosse called "the fascist revolution" combined discontent with modernity, fascination with war
and violence, elements of mass movements and revolutionary

elan with a profoundly reactionary and racist program. In my interpretation of "reactionary modernism," I drew attention to the combination of a fascination with modern technology with a rejection of liberal, political values and institutions within the Nazi party and regime.[6] Flying jet planes into the World Trade Center and the Pentagon to attack "the Zionist-Crusader alliance" and launch oneself on a presumed path to paradise was certainly a reactionary modernist act of the first order. Yet, perhaps because it's origins lie outside Europe, and because its practitioners come from parts of the world endowed with the halo of victimization by the West, there has been a reluctance to acknowledge the links and affinities between fascist mentalities of the past and those of radical Islam. Or, perhaps as in the 1930s and 1940s, the sheer absurdity of radical antisemitism makes it difficult for the educated, largely secular world to believe that anyone could actually believe such things.

Kuentzel points to the irony that the attacks of 9/11, rather than undermining antisemitism, contributed to its diffusion.[7] 9/11, he writes, became an "anti-Semitic signal." Moreover, hostility to Israel and to the Jews has intensified in the Middle East and in Europe in the face of terrorist attacks on civilians in Israel. The unambiguous expressions of Jew-hatred from the Islamists have not aroused the same degree of moral revulsion that would be the case if the source were neo-Nazis in Europe or that would likely emerge in response to open expressions of other forms of racial or religious hatreds. Israel's critics frequently insist that their opposition to Israeli policies or to Zionism itself is not an expression of antisemitism. If that is the case, then why did so many intensify their criticism of Israel as terrorist attacks on Israeli civilians multiplied?[8] Kuentzel's book also implicitly raises the question of whether Jew-hatred has assumed a kind of respectability and acceptance that it had lost in the half century following the Holocaust.[9]

It is the important, and not always pleasant task of intellectual and cultural historians to adopt Kuentzel's "unflinching gaze" at repugnant ideas. While a certain tradition that fashions itself as realist prefers to believe that absurd or irrational views have little impact on the actual world of affairs, or that political actors who voice such views do not really believe in what they are saying, historians of Europe's twentieth century know that some fanatics both believed their wildest fantasies and also acted on them.

Kuentzel's work gives us good grounds to adopt his unflinching gaze and to acknowledge that "Jihad and Jew-hatred belong together." There is much work for scholars to do on the *lineages, similarities and differences* between fascism and Nazism in Europe, on the one hand, and the emergence and development of Islamism in the Middle East, on the other. *Jihad and Jew-Hatred* should stimulate historians of Nazism to expand their comparative, spatial and temporal horizons regarding the aftereffects of Nazism and encourage students of Islam and the Middle East to delve further into this chapter of Europe's influence to understand why it was that radical Islam developed when and where it did. Kuentzel's scholarly and intellectual challenge is also a moral one. He wants to remind all who seek to defeat the threat to civilization posed by radical Islamist terror that, "whoever does not to combat antisemitism, however hasn't the slightest chance of defeating Islamism." This fine work makes a significant contribution to that effort.

Jeffrey Herf, June 3, 2007

Notes

1. *Jihad and Jew-Hatred* builds on the work of students of the interaction of the Arab and Islamic world with Europe during and after World War Two. On the diffusion of ideologies, see Walter Laqueur, *The Changing Face of Anti-Semitism: From Ancient Times to the Present Day* (New York: Oxford University Press, 2006); and Bernard Lewis, *Semites and Anti-Semites: An Inquiry into Conflict and Prejudice* (New York: W.W. Norton, 1986 and 1999). The classic work on Nazi Germany in the Middle East during World War II is Lukasz Hirszowicz, *The Third Reich and the Arab East* (London and Toronto: Routledge and Kegan Paul; University of Toronto Press, 1966). Most recently see Klaus-Michael Mallmann and Martin Cüppers, *Halbmond und Hakenkreuz:Das Dritte Reich, die Araber und Palästina* (Darmstadt: Wissenschaftliche Buchgesellschaft, 2006).

2. On this see Norbert Frei, *Adenauer's Germany and the Nazi Past,* trans. by Joel Golb (New York: Columbia University Press, 2002); Jeffrey Herf, *Divided Memory: The Nazi Past in the Two Germanys* (Harvard University Press, 1997); Tony Judt, *Postwar: A History of Europe Since 1945* (New York: W.W. Norton, 2005); Mark Mazower, *Dark Continent: Europe's Twentieth Century* (New York: Vintage, 2000).

3. Jeffrey Herf, *The Jewish Enemy: Nazi Propaganda During World War II and the Holocaust* (Cambridge, MA: Harvard University Press, 2006).

4. On Qutb's "Our Struggle with the Jews" see Ronald L. Nettler, *Past Trials and Present Tribulations: A Muslim Fundamentalist's View of the Jews* (Oxford: Pergamen Press, 1987).

5. *The 9/11 Commission Report* (New York: W.W. Norton, 2004), pp. 50-51.

6. Jeffrey Herf, *Reactionary Modernism: Technology, Culture and Politics in Weimar and the Third Reich* (New York: Cambridge University Press, 1984).

7. On this response to terrorism, also see Paul Berman, *Terror and Liberalism* (New York: W.W. Norton, 2003).

8. On the blurring lines between anti-Zionism and antisemitism, see Jeffrey Herf, ed., *Antisemitism and Anti-Zionism in Historical Perspective: Convergence and Divergence* (London: Routledge/Taylor and Francis, 2006).

9. On the issue of the respectability of anti-Americanism and anti-Zionism in Europe, see Andrei Markovits, *Uncouth Nation: Why Europe Dislikes America* (Princeton: Princeton University Press, 2006).

PREFACE

· · · · · · · · · ·

The idea of using suicide pilots to obliterate the skyscrapers of Manhattan originated in Berlin. "In the latter stages of the war, I never saw Hitler so beside himself as when, as if in a delirium, he was picturing to himself and to us the downfall of New York in towers of flame," wrote architect Albert Speer in his diary. "He [Hitler] described the skyscrapers turning into huge burning torches and falling hither and thither, and the reflection of the disintegrating city in the dark sky."[1]

Not only Hitler's fantasy but also his plan for realising it, recall what happened in 2001: the idea was for Kamikaze pilots to fly explosive-crammed light aircraft lacking landing gear into the Manhattan skyscrapers. The drawings for the Daimler-Benz "Amerikabomber" from spring 1944 actually exist. They show giant four-engine planes with raised underbellies beneath which small bombers could be strapped. The bombers were to be released shortly before the plane reached the East Coast, after which the mother plane would return to Europe.[2]

The rapture into which Hitler was plunged by the thought of Manhattan in flames indicates the motive behind this fantasy. Hitler did not merely wish to fight a military adversary. He wanted to kill Jews in order to liberate mankind. Possessed by the notion that the whole of the Second World War was a strug-

1. Albert Speer, *Spandauer Tagebücher*, Frankfurt/M. 1975, pp. 126ff. (Entry for November 18, 1947).
2. On the Amerikabomber see: Jochen Thies, 'Bomben auf Manhattan', *Die Zeit*, September 17,2001; Dieter Wulf, 'Die Stunde der Selbstmörder', *Süddeutsche Zeitung*, October 8, 2002; and John K. Cooley, 'Meanwhile: Hitler also plotted to bomb New York', *International Herald Tribune* (IHT), October 24, 2003.

gle against an imaginary Jewish power, he deemed "the USA a Jewish state" and New York the centre of world Jewry.[3] "Wall Street," as a best-seller from the Weimar Republic epoch put it, "is, so to speak, the Military Headquarters of Judas. From there his threads radiate across the entire world."[4] Since 1941 Hitler had been pushing to get the bombers into production, in order to "be able to teach the Jews a lesson in the form of terror attacks on American metropolises." Towards the end of the war this idea became an obsession.

Sixty years later the real assault on the World Trade Centre was coordinated from Germany. 31-year-old Egyptian, Moham-mad Atta, who piloted the Boeing carrying 82 passengers and 11 crew members on board that crashed into the 81st floor of the North Tower of the World Trade Centre, had lived in Germany since 1992. 21-year-old Marwan el-Shehdi from the United Arab Emirates, who piloted a plane with 56 passengers and nine crew members on board into the South Tower, had lived in Germany since 1996, as had 24-year-old Ziad Jarrah from Lebanon, who crashed a Boeing carrying 37 passengers and 7 crew members into a field near Shanksville, Pennsylvania. With Ramzi Binalshibh and Mounir el Motassedeq, they had formed an al-Qa'ida cell in Hamburg where they held regular "Koran circle" meetings with sympathizers.

What ideas propelled Atta and his friends into action? An answer was provided by the witnesses at the world's first 9/11-re-lated trial, that of Motassedeq, which was held between October 2002 and February 2003 in Hamburg. According to a participant in the Koran circle meetings, Said Nickels, "they believed in a Jewish world conspiracy." According to them, "the Second World

---

3. "One can really describe the USA as a Jewish state," wrote Goebbels in April 1943 (from: Jeffrey Herf, *The Jewish Enemy. Nazi Propaganda during World War II and the Holocaust*, (Cambridge MA and London, Harvard University Press 2006), p. 203.
4. Wilhelm Meister, *Judas Schuldbuch. Eine deutsche Abrechnung* (Munich, Deutscher Volksverlag 1919), p. 168.

War had been engineered by the Jews so that they could establish Israel." The head of the World Bank was a Jew, the Jews organized the economic crisis in Asia and "Monica Lewinsky had been sent by the Jews to make a fool out of Clinton." There had been much talk about New York, stated Nickels, "because so many Jews lived there." "They saw that city as the centre of world Jewry."

Motassedeq's house mates confirmed this picture. He had defended Hitler's policy and enthused about a forthcoming "big action." "The Jews will burn and in the end we will dance on their graves."[5] Can we not see an echo of Hitler's rapture in Motassedeq's gleeful anticipation of the "burning Jews?" Despite all the differences between Osama bin Laden's volunteers and Adolf Hitler's Luftwaffe, they obviously share a common feature: antisemitism.

It makes a major difference, however, whether the ideas whose logical conclusion was the Holocaust were adopted before or after the murder of the six million Jews. The Muslim students in Hamburg knew what they were saying and meant it. Amazingly, the American media took almost no notice of this evidence. Had it been the trial of a Ku Klux Klan member or someone from the far right such as the Oklahoma bomber Timothy McVeigh[6] reports of Nazi-like antisemitism would probably have made the headlines. But here, where the attackers were from an Arab background, the international media seemed to find the issue irrelevant: not a single major newspaper reported it.

Moreover, this antisemitism was not only a characteristic of the Hamburg cell, it is shared by Osama bin Laden himself. As the al-Qa'ida leader declared in 1998, "the enmity between us

5. Christian Eggers, 'Die Juden werden brennen' – Die antisemitischen Wahnvorstellungen der Hamburger Al Qaida-Zelle um Mohammed Atta', in *Matthias Küntzel, ,Heimliches Einverständnis'?Islamischer Antisemitismus und deutsche Politik,* forthcoming from LIT-publisher, Münster, Germany, in fall 2007.
6. Timothy McVeigh was the main actor in the most devastating terrorist attack in the USA until that time. On April 19, 1995 he blew up a US Government building in Oklahoma City killing 168 people.

and the Jews goes back far in time and is deep rooted. There is no question that war between us is inevitable…. The Hour of Resurrection shall not come before the Muslims fight Jews." In his view, America is controlled by the Jews. Regarding the Clinton administration, "We believe that this administration represents Israel inside America… The Jews… make use of America to further their plans for the world, especially the Islamic world."[7]

Yet even the 9/11 Commission Report prepared by the National Commission on Terrorist Attacks upon the United States and presented to the public by Republican Thomas H. Kean and his Democrat colleague Lee H. Hamilton in July 2004, makes no mention of bin Laden's antisemitism. In the course of its 584 pages, it lucidly explains what happened when and, with its 1,800 footnotes, is a model of rigor and clarity. It falls short nonetheless, in the two areas on which this book focuses. The first relates to the history of Islamism, which originated in 1928 and engendered al-Qa'ida. The entire pre-1945 period gets five lines. The second is ideological. While the chapter on the Hamburg cell mentions Atta's Jew-hatred,[8] the word antisemitism does not appear at all in the chapter "Bin Laden's worldview." This is all the more surprising in that the Commission quotes documents in which Bin Laden gives unambiguous expression to his antisemitism. One such example is his 'Letter to the American People' of November 2002, which the report repeatedly cites. In this open letter, the al-Qa'ida leader warns, "the Jews have taken control of your media, and now control all aspects

7. Osama bin Laden, 'Frontline interview' (May 1998), see: http://ontology. buffalo.edu/smith//courses01/rrtw/Laden.htm
8. See p. 161: "In his interactions with other students, Atta voiced virulently antisemitic and anti-American opinions, ranging from condemnations of what he described as a global Jewish movement centred in New York City that supposedly controlled the financial world and the media, to polemics against governments of the Arab world." … "Like Atta, by the late 1990s Binalshibh was decrying what he perceived to be a "Jewish world conspiracy" and p. 165: "One of Motassadeq's roommates recalls him referring to Hitler as a 'good man.'"

of your life making you their servants and achieving their aims at your expense." "Your law is the law of rich and wealthy people," he goes on, "behind them stand the Jews who control your policies, media and economy."[9] But the report's authors failed to see the significance of these words and the antisemitic ideology behind them.

By their omission, they unwittingly confirmed the verdict of Yale computer science professor, David Gelernter, who commented in an October 2001 article about Bin Laden's Jew-hatred that, "Americans don't get it: pure, unmotivated hatred of Jews? Pure hatred, on principle? Germans get it very well: such hatred is illogical and incomprehensible. But it exists."[10]

Indeed. My book demonstrates that al-Qa'ida and the other Islamist groups are guided by an antisemitic ideology that was transferred to the Islamic world in the Nazi period. It shows that the Nazis' paranoid worldview and the "fictional reality" that drove their actions rule the minds of the Islamist terrorists and determine their policies today[11] and it draws conclusions about the current global confrontation.

Until September 11, I was not particularly interested in Islamic antisemitism. My main focus was German antisemitism, on the question of what made Auschwitz possible. Daniel J. Goldhagen's ground-breaking study, "Hitler's Willing Executioners", contributed to this interest as did my research into my own family history. For the first time following my father's death in 1996, I was able to read my grandparents' letters from the 1930s

---

9.   "Bin Laden's 'Letter to America', Observer Worldview, November 24, 2002 (translated online at http://observer.guardian.co.uk/worldview/story/0,11581,845725,00.html). The letter is quoted on p. 51 of the Commission Report.
10.   David Gelernter, 'Warum Amerika? Bin Ladens Hass ist Judenhass', Frankfurter Allgemeine Zeitung, October 27, 2001.
11.   For the concept of fictional reality, see Joel Fishman, 'The Big Lie and The Media War Against Israel: From Inversion of the Truth to Inversion of Reality', Jewish Political Studies Review 19, nos. 1 & 2 (Spring 5767/2007), pp. 59-81.

and those sent by my father from the Western Front in 1945, letters from a family that had profited from "Aryanization" and remained loyal to the Nazi regime until the bitter end.

In my 2000 book on the Kosovo war, I consciously avoided the whole area of Islamism and jihad, wishing, as an author with roots in the political left, to avoid if possible terms that might have racist connotations.

On September 11, my avoidance strategy collapsed along with the Twin Towers. I now focused on a single question: why? Hamburg University library is particularly strong on political science and so, on the very first weekend following 9/11 the bulk of the then extant scholarly literature on the origins of Islamism and the Egyptian Muslim Brotherhood, the links to National Socialism, and al-Qa'ida, Hezbollah and Hamas were piled up on my desk. After a year of research, or more accurately, after a year of immersion in what seemed to me, a previously totally strange and incomprehensible world, I published this book.

By then, most of my erstwhile political friends on the left had excluded me from their world-a world that had either greeted 9/11 with unconcealed gloating or interpreted it in an "anti-imperialist" framework, with the wicked USA on the one side and an understandable, if a misguided act of resistance on the other. My 2002 introduction, extracts which are included here, strikes a correspondingly defiant note.

However, the initial response of the wider German public to my book, which explains Islamist terror as a product of a delusional mind set rather than American foreign policy, was also hostile. It was described as "political propaganda," to quote one example from Germany's leading public service radio station, Deutschlandfunk. My book "follows in the slipstream of ultra-conservative warriors for culture and civilization of the Samuel Huntington type." Apparently I had "replaced knowledge with ideas that would be music to the ears of the Bush camp and apologists for current Israeli policy."[12] My critics did not, however, point out any actual errors of fact or failures of logic. In fact, the first expert in the field to publicly defend and recommend my book was a Muslim, the Syrian-born political scientist Bassam Tibi.

The book attracted far more interest between historians and scholars of antisemitism in other parts of the world, especially the USA. I was invited to lecture at Yale University (New Haven, Ct.), Brown University (Providence, R.I.), and Penn State University (State College, PA) and the book was discussed in magazines such as the *New Republic* and *Telos*. In 2004, I became an external research assistant at the Vidal Sassoon International Center for the Study of Antisemitism at the Hebrew University of Jerusalem and have lectured in Israel. It was only via this detour that the book began to get a more positive hearing in Germany. I would therefore, at this point like to thank my many American and Israeli friends and colleagues for their many forms of support and encouragement, in particular Omer Bartov, Phyllis Chesler, Joel Fishman, Manfred Gerstenfeld, Daniel Goldhagen, Jeffrey Herf, Judith Jacobsen, Dori Laub, Andrei Markovits, Eldad Pardo, Marty Peretz, John Rosenthal, Charles Small and Robert Wistrich. Special thanks go to Russell Berman, who first made the American edition of this book possible and my translator Colin Meade. The body of the book has been translated from the 2002 German edition, with a few additions to take into account works that have appeared since 2002. Regrettably, the past five years have confirmed the pessimistic prognosis I made in 2002. I address some aspects of the current situation in my postscript.

Matthias Küntzel, May 1, 2007

12. As for example Christoph Burgmer in his broadcast review on *Deutschlandfunk*, January 6, 2003.

INTRODUCTION
. . . .

University graduates who blow themselves up with the aim of heavenly self-improvement, priests who throw hydrochloric acid into young women's faces to punish them for violating the obligation to wear the veil, parents who cheerfully prepare their children for *jihad* with dummy explosive belts, anyone seeking to find the motives for such behaviour enters a world in which reason is considered betrayal, doubt a deadly sin and the Jews "the brothers of monkeys, murderers of the Prophet, blood-suckers and warmongers."

Many people, not wishing to suffer the vertigo induced by this reality, prefer to cling to what they are used to. This begins with the assessment of the suicidal mass murders of Israeli civilians. The perpetrators' videos, recordings of their last will and testament, show proud and enthusiastic men, genuinely keen to blow themselves up and kill as many Jews as possible in the process. The "well-educated" observer, however, does not want either to see or acknowledge this enthusiasm, insisting instead that the murderers are motivated by hopelessness and despair. The question of why it is, that nowhere else do people draw the conclusion from their desperate state that they should blow themselves up in crowded buses or restaurants does not occur to them. Any fact or question inconsistent with the imperative requirement for inner tranquillity is suppressed.

Since September 11, 2001, the efforts to ward off reality have been taken to a new level. A few months after the attack, one of Osama bin Laden's closest associates announced that "Al-Qa'ida takes pride in the fact that, on 11 September, it destroyed ele-

1

ments of America's strategic defence." But it made no difference as the jihadi responsibility for the mass murder in New York and Washington became clearer, all the more maniacally did the right-thinking fall back on their tried-and-tested frameworks, pointing the finger of suspicion at the CIA or other American state agencies. Months after al-Qa'ida had laid claim to the attack, a left-wing newspaper described the notion that it bore sole responsibility for September 11 as the "biggest of all conspiracy theories" belonging to the realm of fantasy, thus enabling it to pursue undeflected the search for circumstantial evidence of "the possible interest of the ruling circles [in the US] in a trigger event for a global campaign."

This book takes a different path. It is based on the conviction that anyone wishing to get closer to an understanding of jihadism must leave the cosy fireside of the accustomed and accept insights which may send a shiver down the spine, but which nonetheless have to be spelt out. It differs from most other writings on Islamism first and foremost because it acknowledges its anti-Jewish program. The unusualness of this is clear from the treatment given to the Charter of the Islamist movement Hamas. Although all the motives for Hamas' anti-Jewish war can be found there, it is never referred to in discussions regarding the motives of the suicide bombers. In the Hamas Charter not only are the Jews, in Nazi style, held responsible for the French and Russian Revolutions, they are also blamed for the First and Second World Wars. The United Nations is exposed as an instrument of Jewish plans for world domination. To support these accusations, the most notorious of all antisemitic forgeries, the *Protocols of the Elders of Zion*, is cited.

Secondly, while many writers have surrendered to the "fascination" of Islamism to the point they believe they can deduce its progressive nature and historic legitimacy from its mass character, this book takes the view that a mass movement which considers itself revolutionary can be of a thoroughly fascist nature. The example of National Socialism shows that an ostensibly anti-capitalist revolutionary movement can be both antisemitic and fascist at the same time.

Thirdly, the development of Islamism is treated here as inseparable from its social context, as an ideological and cultural response to specific political and economic conditions.

At the centre of this study lies the most important Islamist movement, the Muslim Brotherhood, founded in Egypt in 1928. This movement in the context of the world economic crisis, rediscovered the idea of military jihad and the search for death as the guiding ideal of the martyr. The Muslim Brothers lie behind Hamas, the most important Palestinian jihadi organization. The links between the Brotherhood in Palestine and Osama bin Laden's Al-Qa'ida have been especially close throughout. It was a founding member of Hamas, Abdullah Azzam, who first introduced bin Laden to the jihadi philosophy in the 1980s.

Despite frequent assertions to the contrary, the Muslim Brothers were inspired not by the Nasserism of the 1960s, but by the European fascism of the 1930s. Their pre-1951 campaigns were not anti-colonialist, but anti-Jewish. The anti-Jewish passages in the Koran were fused with the antisemitic methods of struggle of the Third Reich and hatred of the Jews acted out as jihad.

Six months after the end of the Nazi regime, the Muslim Brotherhood provoked the greatest anti-Jewish riots in Egyptian history, an event which heralded the shift of the centre of antisemitism from Germany to the Arab world.

However, it was after the end of the Cold War that the Muslim Brothers' jihad sprang back to life in Palestine. Since 1994 it has escalated in the form of suicidal mass murders of Israeli civilians.

Then came September 11. In hindsight, the massacres in New York and Washington proved to be a pointer to the future. Firstly, Islamism would henceforth be the vanguard of an anti-

Americanism imbued with Jew-hatred. Secondly, it gave a new boost to antisemitism; the deadly force of the attacks rebounded in the first place onto Israel. In the subsequent weeks, Israel saw itself confronted not only by an escalation of Palestinian suicide bombings, but also by antisemitic mobilizations in Europe and the Arab world.

When in April 2002 well over two million people came into the streets in the capitals of the Arab world to urge on the suicide bombers of Israeli civilians, the potential for a new anti-Jewish and anti-American rebellion was manifested for the first time. A rebellion which, instead of anti-colonialism and emancipation, inscribes antisemitism and oppression on its banner; a rebellion driven by religious frenzy rather than objective reason, but which at the same time in terms of the numbers mobilized pales against all other anti-western revolutions.

The new movement's leadership is made up not of religiously inflamed peasants, but calculating strategists. The measure of their destructive intelligence can be gauged by anyone who takes note of the Hamas Charter.

"It is necessary to study conscientiously the enemy and its material and human potential; to detect its weak and strong spots, and to recognise the powers that support it and stand by it. At the same time, we must be aware of the current events, follow the news and study the analyses and commentaries on it, together with drawing up plans for the present and the future and examining every phenomenon." In line with this approach, leading al-Qa'ida officials issued documents painstakingly comparing the impact of September 11 with the results of the Munich Olympic attack of 1972 or defining the tactical relationship between Islamism and the anti-globalization movement.

It is this combination of anti-Jewish delirium and rational methodology which has made Islamism the most successful movement of the past ten years.

Hunger, oppression and underdevelopment may be the breeding ground for a terrorism of despair. In the case of the Islamists of Hamas or Al-Qa'ida, however, we are not dealing with desperate people, spontaneously responding to immediate economic pressures. These are faith-driven warriors, people with a rigorously worked-out ideological program who project all the world's evils onto Israel and the "Jew-dominated" USA.

These delusions have little to do with any specific Western policy. In Islamist eyes, not only is everything Jewish evil, all evil is Jewish. The USA is not attacked for what it does, but for what it is: the centre of a type of society based on political and religious freedom.

Insofar as Islamism relates to genuine injustices in the world, it is obvious that there are two possible answers as to how such injustices should be remedied, responses which are in no way compatible. Firstly, the enlightenment-based and emancipatory response that seeks to establish a more humane society, building on the achievements of modernity to do so. And, secondly, the reactionary and antisemitic approach, which identifies particular manifestations of capitalism, notably the principle of individualism and commerce, with "the Jews" in the broadest sense and wants to "liberate" itself through their destruction.

But it is the state of this world that guarantees new life for the antisemitic rebellion. The combination of worldly fantasies and the promise of other worldly salvation increases its destructive force. Those who want to find rational grounds for criticizing the political approach adopted towards, and the military measures taken against, jihadism, must first adequately analyze the object in question. This however, presupposes an unflinching gaze. This book is aimed at assisting in this process.

Hamburg, September 1, 2002

CHAPTER ONE
. . . .
THE MUSLIM BROTHERHOOD AND PALESTINE

On November 2, 1917 the British government, through its Foreign Minister, Lord Balfour, announced its support for the establishment in Palestine of a national home for the Jewish people. The Balfour Declaration has since then been accepted as the starting point for the Jewish-Arab conflict.

This view, however, overlooks the fact that important representatives of the Arab world of the day supported the Zionist settlement process. They hoped that Jewish immigration would boost economic development thus bringing the Middle East closer to European levels. For example, Ziwar Pasha, later Egyptian Prime Minister, personally took part in the celebrations of the Balfour Declaration in 1917. Five years later Ahmed Zaki, a former Egyptian cabinet minister, congratulated the Zionist Executive in Palestine on its progress: "The victory of the Zionist idea is the turning point for the fulfilment of an ideal which is so dear to me, the revival of the Orient." Two years later the Chairman of the Zionist Executive, Frederick H. Kisch, travelled to Cairo for talks with three high-ranking Egyptian officials on future relations. These officials "were equally emphatic in their pro-Zionist declarations", noted Kisch in his diary. All three "recognized that the progress of Zionism might help to secure the development of a new Eastern civilization." In 1925 the Egyptian Interior Minister Ismail Sidqi took action against a group of Palestinians protesting against the Balfour Declaration in Cairo. He was at the time on his way to Jerusalem to take part in the open-ing of the first Hebrew university.[13]

Twenty years later scarcely anything remained of this benev-olent attitude. In 1945 the worst anti-Jewish pogroms in Egypt's history were perpetrated in Cairo. On November 2, 1945, on the anniversary of the Balfour Declaration, demonstrators "broke into the Jewish quarter, plundered houses and shops, attacked non-Muslims, and devastated the adjacent Ashkenazi synagogue before finally setting it on fire." The event left some 400 peo-ple injured and a policeman dead. Meanwhile in Alexandria, at least five people were killed in the course of even more violent riots "which according to a British embassy official were clearly anti-Jewish and, to his relief, not directed against the British." A few weeks later Islamist newspapers "launched a frontal attack against Egypt's Jews as being Zionists, Communists, capitalists, bloodsuckers, traffickers in arms, white slave-traders and, more generally, a 'subversive element' in all states and societies", and called for a boycott of Jewish goods.[14]

In the following sections, we shall look at the reasons why, between 1925 and 1945, a shift in direction was effected in Egypt from a rather neutral or pro-Jewish mood to a rabidly anti-Zi-onist or anti-Jewish one, a shift which changed the whole Arab world and affects it to this day. The driving force behind this development was the "Society of Muslim Brothers" (*Gamiyyat al-ikhwan al-muslimin*), founded in 1928. The significance of this organization goes far beyond Egypt. For today's global Islamist movement the Muslim Brothers are what the Bolsheviks were for

---

13. See Abd Al-Fattah Muhammad Al-Awaisi, *The Muslim Brothers and the Palestine Question 1928-1947* (London: Tauris Academic Studies, 1998) pp. 22 and 69, and Frederick H. Kisch, *Palestine Diary* (London: Gollancz Ltd., 1938), pp. 109ff. Among the prominent Egyptians involved were Aziz Bey Ali (alias Aziz al-Misri, who in 1939 was appointed head of the Egyptian armed forces), Hasan Sabri (named head of the government in 1940) and Sayyid Ka-mil Pasha, a son of the former Grand Visier of the Sultan, Abd al-Hamid.
14. Gudrun Krämer, *Minderheit, Millet, Nation? Die Juden in Ägypten 1914-1952* (Wiesbaden: Verlag Otto Harrassowitz, 1982), pp 320ff and 408.

the Communist movement of the 1920s: the ideological reference point and organizational core which decisively inspired all the subsequent tendencies and continues to do so to this day.

The Islamist Vanguard

The Egyptian situation in the 1920s was marked by multifaceted social changes. In the First World War, with British help, the Arab elites had defeated the Ottoman despotism. In 1924 the last Caliphate of Istanbul was abolished. European ideologies such as liberalism and nationalism met with a positive response in Egypt's leading circles, literature began to follow European models, scholarship began to open up to Western influences and Egyptian women took off their headscarves.[15]

The independence which Britain had promised its former colony in 1922, had however, never been fully granted and relations were stretched to the breaking point. National resistance to British imperialism was further fuelled by social conflicts. The First World War had unleashed an industrial and employment boom, which collapsed with the war's end. Industrial action ensued in Cairo, Alexandria and the Canal Zone. The world economic crisis exacerbated the already tense situation. Between 1928 and 1931 the world price for cotton, Egypt's most important export, fell from 26 to 10 dollars per unit.

It was against this culturally, politically and socially agitated background that in March 1928 the charismatic preacher Hassan al-Banna founded the Muslim Brotherhood with six employees of the Suez Canal Company. After a period of cadre training, the Brotherhood "grew from insignificance and mediocrity to the largest group in the whole of the Near and Middle East, capable of exerting a great deal of pressure upon public opinion and

---

15. Israel Gershoni, James P. Jankowski, *Redefining the Egyptian Nation 1930-1945* (Cambridge UK: Cambridge University Press, 1995), pp. 2ff.

government circles."[16] Its membership rose from 800 in 1936 to 200,000 in 1938, to reach its highpoint of 500,000 members, with 2,000 sub-units and some 500,000 sympathisers, in 1948.[17] At that time, its paramilitary wing alone, established to carry out an armed Islamic uprising, had 40,000 members.[18]

On the one hand, this was a religious movement. Following his teachers Muhammad Abduh and Rashid Rida, al-Banna advocated a return to early Islam as the only true religion, and as such destined to supremacy. In his view, contemporary Islam had lost this social dominance, because most Muslims had become corrupted by Western influence and seduced into surrendering their religiosity. The Koran and Sunna had equipped Muslims with God-given laws valid for all time and all spheres of life - from problems of everyday life to the organization of states and the world. For al-Banna, only a return to orthodox Islam could pave the way for an end to the intolerable conditions and humiliations of Muslims and newly establish the righteous Islamic order.[19]

At the same time, the Muslim Brothers were also a revolutionary political movement and as such in many respects trailblazers. The Brotherhood was the first Islamic organization to put down roots in the cities and organize as a mass movement. Unlike other Salifist reformers, al-Banna was a populist and activist, not an elitist.[20] The Brotherhood put itself forward as the representative of the interests of the workers against the tyranny of foreign and monopoly owners. A committee for the unemployed was founded, the employment of British workers combated and a community of interests between Egyptian labour

16.   J. Heyworth-Dunne, *Religious and Political Trends In Modern Egypt*, Published by the author, Washington 1950, p. 68.
17.   El-Awaisi, op. cit., p. 98 and Richard P. Mitchell, *The Society of the Muslim Brothers* (London: Oxford University Press, 1969), p. 328.
18.   Richard P. Mitchell, op. cit., p. 14.
19.   Mitchell, op. cit., p. 203; *sunna* refers to the collection of the sayings and doings of the Prophet, later established as legally binding precedents.
20.   Salafism (*as-salaf as-salih* = the pious forefathers) is the term used for the ideal of a return to the early Islam of the seventh century.

and capital sought. Wherever Egyptian hospitals, pharmacies or schools were lacking the Brotherhood stepped in. It offered loans to the needy and established its own industrial enterprises for the unemployed whose structures, by presenting an alternative to the exploitative practices of other workplaces, were intended to demonstrate the advantages of an Islamic economy.

In addition, the Brotherhood was the first Islamist movement that systematically set about building a kind of "Islamist international." To this end, it purposefully recruited foreign students in Cairo in order to create the backbone of branches in other countries, such as Lebanon (1936), Syria (1937) and Transjordan (1946). In 1940 it set up the Palestine and Islamic World Committee, comprised of the Near East Committee (Arab world and Africa, Turkey and Iran), Far East Committees (Afghanistan, Turkmenistan, China, India, Indonesia and Japan) and Europe committee. The Cairo headquarters of the *Ikhwan* (Brotherhood) was expanded into a centre and meeting place for representatives of the whole Islamic world.[21]

What were the main points of the *ikhwans'* revolutionary program? Tightly organized according to the leadership principle, it demanded the dissolution of all parties and the abolition of parliamentary democracy in favour of an "organic" state based on *sharia* law and the Caliphate. No political current was more fiercely opposed than the Communist Party, denounced as "foreign." When the Communist Party's influence rose in 1946, the Brotherhood devoted a daily column in its newspaper to the "Fight against Communism", infiltrated members of its secret service into the Communist Party and handed over the latter's members to the state security organs.[22]

On the economic front, it called for the abolition of interest and profit and propagated a community of interests between labour and capital. While finance and interest-bearing capital,

21. El-Awaisi, op. cit., pp. 138ff.
22. Mitchell, op. cit., p. 39.

perceived as the mysterious and abstract side of capitalism, were declared the root of all evil, its seemingly concrete man-ifestations-machines, factories and labour discipline-were glorified. In addition, the use of "Western" science and the most advanced technology was propagated as the precondition for military supremacy and Islamic world rule. The Brotherhood's list of demands in 1952 were; (1) A ban on interest and closure of the stock exchange; (2) nationalization of natural resources; (3) a crash industrialization program with priority for military industries and industrial branches which could be supplied from domestic sources; (4) nationalization of the banks; (5) land reform through expropriation of large land holdings; and (6) social security for workers and the unemployed.[23]

But at the forefront of the Brotherhood's efforts lay the struggle against all the sensual and "materialistic" temptations of the capitalist and communist world. At the tender age of 13, the pubescent al-Banna had founded a "Society for the Prevention of the Forbidden"[24] and this is in essence what the Brothers were and are - a community of male zealots, whose primary concern is to prevent all the sensual and sexual sins forbidden according to their interpretation of the Koran. Their signature was most clearly apparent when they periodically reduced their local night clubs, brothels and cinemas - constantly identified with Jewish influence - to ashes.

While it is not possible here to shed light on the issue of the origins of "pleasure in un-pleasure" and how libido can, para-doxically, be linked to its own repression, the point at least needs to be made that the Muslim Brothers were projecting their own libidinal wishes and fantasies onto the unbelievers. Projection is a defence mechanism where the subject makes others responsi-ble for his own rejected or denied feelings and desires. As part of this process, the aggression with which the Muslim Brothers

23. Mitchell, op. cit., pp. 272ff.
24. El-Awaisi, op. cit., p. 118.

denied their own sensual needs had to be worked off in the form of hatred of "Western decadence" and "Jewish amorality"; the only permitted way of drawing closer to the prohibited objects of desire was to destroy them.

Gripped by this phobia, the Society of Muslim Brothers, from the day of its foundation, at the same time provided a haven for any man dedicated to the restoration of male supremacy; the Brotherhood was almost 100% male. Al-Banna had, admittedly, founded a society of "Muslim Sisters", recognizable by their white headscarves. This was a weak sector within the organizational structure, however, and in the 1930s and 40s it was shunned by the majority of Western-educated Egyptian women; it never had more than 5,000 members.[25]

At the start of the 1920s, Egyptian women had founded an independent and influential section in the united party of the national independence movement, the Wafd. In 1923, the president of the Egyptian Women's Rights Union, Huda Sharawi, demonstratively threw her headscarf into the sea.[26] In the same year Mustafa Kemal, who bore the honorific name Atatürk (Father of the Turks) and supported women's equality, founded Turkey. "Nothing in our religion requires women to be subordinate to men", declared the modern Muslim Atatürk. He abolished polygamy, decreed legal equality, opposed the headscarf and ensured that his adopted daughter was able to have a career as a pilot and, indeed, that a Muslim aristocratic woman could have one as an actress.[27]

At the very time when the liberation of women from the inferiority decreed by Islam was gradually getting under way, the Muslim Brotherhood set itself up as the rallying point for the restoration of patriarchal domination: for is it not written in the

25. See Mitchell, op. cit., pp. 175 and 254ff.
26. Naila Minai, *Schwestern unterm Halbmond. Muslimische Frauen zwischen Tradition und Emanzipation* (Munich: Klett-Cotta, 1989), p. 82.
27. Naila Minai, op. cit., pp. 76ff and Eberhard Serauky, *Im Namen Allahs. Der Terrorismus im Nahen Osten* (Berlin: Dietz, 2000), pp. 99ff.

Koran that "men are in charge of women" (sura 4, verse 34) and "stand a step above women (sura 2, verse 228)?"

According to the *ikhwans'* reading of the Koran, women must not leave their homes unless clad from head to toe in opaque garments. Late marriage and contraception were frowned upon. Divorce was strictly rejected and polygamy for men allowed, although in practice restricted to cases of female infertility, illness or "insanity." Public association of men and women was as a rule not allowed. While in the Brotherhood's code men were considered potential leadership material, women's allotted "natural" destiny was the home, the family and above all the raising of male children. Employment for women was only permissible in cases of dire necessity and was concentrated in the areas of education and health care. The education of girls was to focus primarily on preparing them for their "natural" role as mother and wife. The denial of female sexuality and the idealization of the mother's role went hand in hand. Among al-Banna's first projects was an Institute for the Mothers of Believers, later converted into the headquarters of the "Muslim Sisters."

The Brotherhood's most significant innovation was their concept of jihad as holy war, which significantly differed from other contemporary doctrines and, associated with that, the passionately pursued goal of dying a martyr's death in the war with the unbeliever. Before the founding of the Brotherhood, Islamic currents of modern times had understood jihad (derived from a root signifying "effort") as the individual striving for belief or the missionary task of disseminating Islam. Only when this missionary work was hindered were they allowed to use force to defend themselves against the unbelievers' resistance. The starting point of Islamism is the new interpretation of jihad, espoused with uncompromising militancy by Hassan al-Banna, the first to preach this kind of jihad in modern times.[28] "What concerns

28. Bassam Tibi, *Fundamentalismus in Islam. Eine Gefahr für den Weltfrieden?* (Darmstadt: Wissenschaftliche Buchgesellschaft, 2000a), p. 117; Ibid., *Die*

us here about this new understanding is the concept of jihad, which had been almost absent from Islamic education before the foundation of the Muslim Brothers...[p]olitical parties were involved with political struggles and mosque Imams and preachers treated jihad as irrelevant to their religious brief" emphasises El-Awaisi in his study.[29]

On the "Art of Death"

The jihad motif is, for example, central to the Muslim Brothers' emblem, which displays the first two words of a verse of the Koran extolling jihad surrounded by two swords. The same note is struck by the Brotherhood's founding manifesto, reiterated at every opportunity: "Allah is our goal, the prophet our model, the Koran our constitution, the Jihad our path and death for the sake of Allah the loftiest of our wishes."[30]

In 1938, in a leading article entitled "Industry of Death," which was to become famous, Hassan al-Banna explained to a wider public his concept of jihad - a concept in which the term Industry of Death denotes not something horrible but an ideal. He wrote: "to a nation that perfects the industry of death and which knows how to die nobly, God gives proud life in this world and eternal grace in the life to come."[31]

According to al-Banna, the Koran enjoins believers to love death more than life. Unfortunately, he argues, Muslims are in

neue Weltordnung. Westliche Dominanz und islamischer Fundamentalismus (Munich, 2001a), pp. 134ff.
29. El-Awaisi, op. cit., p. 124.
30. Franz Kogelmann, Die Islamisten Ägyptens in der Regierungszeit von Anwar as-Sadat (1970-1981) (Berlin: Klaus Schwarz Verlag, 1994), p. 29 and El-Awaisi, op. cit., p. 125.
31. The praise for the nation which knows "how to die nobly" is highly topical. Hamas, as the Muslim Brothers' organization in Palestine is known, has explained the success of their suicidal mass murder strategy by the distinction enunciated by al-Banna: unlike those who have mastered the art of death, the weakness of "the Jews" lies precisely in the fact that "they love life more than any other people and prefer not to die", as Hamas spokesman Ismail Haniya put it at the time of the 2002 Easter massacres to the Washington Post. See Thomas Friedman, "Suicidal Lies" in New York Times (NYT), 31 March 2002.

thrall to a "love of life." "The illusion which had humiliated us is no more than the love of worldly life and the hatred of death." As long as the Muslims do not replace their love of life with the love of death as required by the Koran, their future is hopeless. Only those who become proficient in the "art of death" can prevail. "So, prepare yourself to do a great deed. Be keen on dying and life will be granted to you, so work towards a noble death and you will win complete happiness," he writes in the same essay,[32] republished in 1946 under the title "The Art of Death."

These notions struck a deep chord, at least with the "troops of God" as the Muslim Brothers liked to be known. Whenever their cohorts marched in close formation through the streets of Cairo, their voices rang out with this song: "We are afraid not of death but we desire it.... How wonderful death is.... Let us die in redemption for Muslims" followed by the chorus; "jihad is our course of action.... and death in the cause of God our most precious wish."[33]

Even at that time, subjective despair over the circumstances of life could not account for a "most precious wish" of this kind, however much people who yearn for an apparently rational explanation may wish it to do so. The Brothers utterly rejected jihad for "material or selfish aims" as contrary to the Koran.[34] Thus the Brotherhood's jihadism never served to improve the material lot of those preparing for martyrdom; its purpose was the struggle against an enemy branded as absolutely evil. But who was this absolute enemy? Not - and this is absolutely amazing - the British who were interfering in Egypt, but the Jews who were migrating to Palestine. And this despite the fact that the Jews in Egypt had a rather good reputation.

32. Quoted in El-Awaisi, op. cit., p. 125. See also Mitchell, op. cit., p. 207.
33. El-Awaisi, op. cit., pp. 125ff.
34. El-Awaisi, op. cit., p. 12.

Anti-German Boycott

The Egyptian revolution of 1919 united all the country's religious groups around the watchwords "Liberty, Equality, Brotherhood." The secular constitution of 1923 devoted not a single word to supranational religious allegiances. With its promulgation, Egypt became a constitutional monarchy.[35] The domestic political conflicts of the subsequent decades were dominated by two power centres: firstly the Wafd Party - the united party of the Egyptian independence movement - which won every election from 1922 to 1952. It took Western democracy as its model and sought a kind of junior partnership with Britain. Its most important parliamentary competitor was the Constitutional Liberal Party, which more strongly represented the interests of the agricultural bourgeoisie.[36] The second power centre was the royal palace, which was ruled by King Fuad (1917-1936) and his pro-German-inclined successor Farouk (1937-1952).

Until the assumption of office by Farouk, the Jews of Egypt were an accepted and protected part of public life: they had members of parliament, were employed at the royal palace and occupied important positions in the economic and political spheres. Joseph Qatawwi, appointed Finance Minister in 1924, was a Jew as was Léon Castro, who in 1917 established the Egyptian section of the International Zionist Organization and in the 1920s was not only the private secretary of Prime Minister Zaghlul, but also the spokesman of the Wafd Party. The Constitutional Liberal Party, the media and the general population were also favourable to the Jews. "It merits emphasis", reported a Viennese journalist, "that the Jewish shopkeeper and commission agent enjoy great popularity with the domestic population and

35. Krämer op. cit., p.253. The trigger for the disturbances later dubbed the "revolution of 1919" was the British refusal to permit an Egyptian delegation (=Wafd) to attend the Versailles peace conference.
36. Joel Beinin, Zachary Lockman, *Workers on the Nile. Nationalism, Communism, Islam and the Egyptian Working Class 1882-1954*, (Princeton NJ: Princeton University Press, 1987) p. 13.

are mostly considered to be very honest."[37] This certainly does merit emphasis! While the everyday antisemitism of Vienna and the rest of Europe had inherited the money lender and Shylock fantasy-images of Christian anti-Judaism, Egyptians were relatively free from such prejudices.

The Zionist movement was likewise accepted impartially. The lack of emotion regarding Palestine was dictated by two considerations: despite the fact that Egypt and Palestine are only divided by the Sinai Peninsula and that Jerusalem and Cairo are a mere 400 km apart, in the first third of the twentieth century the notion that the fate of Egypt might have anything to do with that of some kind of wider Arab world appeared absurd. In 1931, the British High Commissioner, Percy Loraine, optimistically noted that the country was too isolated from the rest of the Arab world to be drawn into pan-Arab or pan-Islamic movements.[38] Moreover, the Egyptian government did its utmost to avoid anything that might impair good relations between the three most important religious groups - Muslims, Jews and Christian Copts.

Not only was Palestine a peripheral concern for Egyptian public opinion and a non-issue for the Egyptian government in the 1920s, but "considerable sympathy was shown by some Egyptian publicists and politicians for the Jewish National Home emerging in Palestine."[39] Thus in 1926 the Egyptian government extended a cordial welcome to a Jewish teachers association delegation from the British mandate territory. Later, students from the Egyptian University travelled on an official visit to Tel Aviv to take part in a sports competition there. When the conflict in Palestine escalated in 1929, the Egyptian Interior Ministry ordered

37. El-Awaisi, op. cit., p. 68. What the Viennese journalist noted in 1904 remained the case in subsequent decades, according to Gudrun Krämer, op. cit., p. 158.
38. Egypt, according to Loraine, "never displayed great enthusiasm for the Islamist movement." See El-Awaisi, op. cit., p. 26
39. James Jankowski, "Egyptian Responses to the Palestine Problem in the Interwar Period", *International Journal of Middle East Studies*, Vol. 12 (1980), p. 4.

its press office to censor all anti-Zionist and pro-Palestinian articles. In December 1930 the Egyptian government sent dozens of Palestinians who had fled to Egypt following the crushing of their "revolt" back to the mandate territory. Various Egyptian figures are reported to have met with Zionist leaders during the decade "apparently declaring their sympathy with Zionism or committing themselves to work for Arab-Jewish 'understanding' in Palestine."[40] Even in 1933, the Egypt government allowed 1,000 new Jewish immigrants to land in Port Said on their way to Palestine.[41]

The assumption of power by the Nazis in Germany sparked massive protests led by the 70-80,000 strong Jewish community, but supported by other sections of the population as well. In March and April 1933 anti-Nazi mass meetings were held in many Egyptian cities. German products and firms that dealt in German goods were systematically boycotted and the showing of German films in Cairo cinemas was prevented by militant action. In the same year Jewish businessmen, lawyers and organizations such as the B'nai B'rith formed a "League against German Antisemitism" which had 1,500 members and coordinated the anti-German protests.[42]

The German Reich and its agents in Egypt were anything but delighted by this mood. In 1926 Alfred Hess, brother of Hitler's deputy-to-be Rudolf Hess, whose family had lived in Alexandria since 1865, formed the *Landesgruppe Ägypten* (Egyptian section) of the NSDAP/AO (the Nazi party organization abroad) with a few hundred members. In response to the boycott of

---

40. Jankowski, op. cit.
41. See El-Awaisi, op. cit., pp. 22ff.
42. Krämer op.cit., pp 261ff, Albrecht Fuess, "Propaganda at the Pyramids: The German Community in Egypt 1919-1939", in Wageh Atik, Wolfgang G. Schwanitz (eds.), *Ägypten und Deutschland im 19. und 20. Jahrhundert im Spiegel der Archivalien* (Cairo: Dar ath-Thaqafa, 1998), pp. 111ff; the subsequent remarks are based on these sources. In September 1933 the Liga joined the Ligue internationale contre l'antisémitisme allemand (LICA), whose vice-president Léon Castro became. See Krämer, op. cit., p. 263.

German goods the Nazi representatives in Cairo organized the distribution of French and German copies of the booklet *Judenfrage in Deutschland* ("The Jewish Question in Germany.") An Italian-Jewish businessman swiftly responded with a legal action charging dissemination of racial hatred and disturbance of public order. Even the German attempt to set up an Arabic press service initially met with failure.[43] "The level of education of the broad masses is not advanced enough for the understanding of race theory", declared a spokesman for the Cairo Nazis in justification. "An understanding of the Jewish threat has not yet been awakened here."[44]

Attention therefore began to be focused on influencing the Egyptian government. The decisive means of pressure was the country's most important export, cotton. Via the German textile industry association, the Nazis threatened to boycott Egyptian cotton in the future. This threat was enough. The Egyptian government criticized the anti-German boycott movement and promised to introduce harsher measures against Egypt's Jews.[45] Even in the Egyptian press, the Jews were increasingly pilloried as wreckers of the Egyptian economy in light of the German threat.

Next, the Nazis made an issue of principle out of the Cairo court case against *Judenfrage in Deutschland*. In Berlin a special joint meeting of the propaganda and foreign ministries was arranged to deal with what it described as the *Judenprozess von Kairo* ("Cairo Jew trial.") In secret meetings with the German embassy, the Egyptian government promised to support the German defence against the Jewish-inspired charges. When the charges were rejected in the courts of first and second instance in 1934 and 1935 respectively, the German media hailed these events as major successes. The anti-German boycott movement

43. Krämer, op. cit., pp. 260 and 298; Fuess, op.cit., p. 102.
44. Krämer, op. cit., p. 278.
45. Fuess, op. cit., p. 114.

fizzled out. In the same year the German Reich opened a branch of the German News Agency in Cairo. Three years later Germany had become the second largest importer of Egyptian goods.

The economic upswing in Nazi Germany and the disciplined mass marches organized by the Nazis increasingly caught the attention of and impressed the Egyptian public. Paramilitary rallies by the pro-fascist Young Egypt movement founded in 1933, the Young Men's Muslim Association (YMMA) and the Muslim Brotherhood increasingly dominated the street-scene, announcing the advent of a third centre of influence in Egyptian politics alongside the Palace and Parliament. Growing public sympathy for the Third Reich - Britain's most important opponent - was initially motivated primarily by anti-British feeling and only marginally by anti-Jewish sentiments. But a change would take place very soon in this respect too.

Anti-Jewish Jihad

In October 1933, when the Jewish-led anti-German boycott movement was still going strong, the Cairo Nazi group discussed the reasons for the failure of their anti-Jewish campaign to date. How could "the broad masses" be awakened to an understanding of the "Jewish threat?" In their report to the Foreign Office in Berlin they drew the conclusion that the value of publicity campaigns "for the creation of an anti-Jewish mood among the Arab population is relatively small" and that "we must therefore focus far more on the point where real conflicts of interest between Arabs and Jews exist: Palestine. The conflict between Arabs and Jews there must be transplanted to Egypt."[46]

The situation in Palestine was indeed more polarized. Not only did a real conflict exist between Arabs and Zionists over immigration and land purchases, but this conflict also offered an opportunity for escalation in a direction pleasing to the Nazis -

46. Krämer, op. cit., p. 278 and Fuess, op. cit., p. 112.

the Palestinian Arab movement was, after all, led by the Mufti of Jerusalem, whose hatred of the Jews was scarcely inferior to that of the Nazis.

It was, however, not until 1936 that the Palestinian dispute would ignite the spark that would kindle the "conflict of interests between Arabs and Jews", as the Nazis put it, in Egypt. The occasion was provided by the Nazis themselves. As the flood of refugees provoked by the German Reich increased the number of Jewish migrants to new levels, the Palestinian Arab reaction was not long in coming. In April 1936 the Mufti called for an Arab general strike against Jewish immigration and British mandate policy in Palestine. We shall return to these disturbances which have gone down in history as the "Arab revolt of 1936-39."

This strike gave the Muslim Brothers the green light to launch their first fanatical solidarity campaign, in which the idea of jihad was linked to the clashes in Palestine. Only now did the Brotherhood become a mass organization, growing between 1936 and 1938 from 800 to 200,000 members.

In May 1936 the Muslim Brothers called for a boycott of the businesses of Egyptian Jews. The Central Committee for Aid to Palestine established by Al-Banna developed into the Brotherhood's stronghold and the centre of its new mission. Pro-Palestinian fund-raising and anti-Jewish boycott campaigns, leafleting and demonstrations were now organized.[47] In mosques, schools and workplaces the Brotherhood worked up the believers with the legend that the Jews and British wished to destroy the holy places of Jerusalem and tear up the Koran and trample it underfoot. Yet initially, these activities encountered strong opposition precisely among the Egyptian religious establishment. In 1936, the Muslim Brothers' efforts to politicize Friday prayers in the mosques "met with a lot of resistance on the part of the mosque imams, who tried to stop them physically or have

47. Krämer, op. cit., pp. 290ff and El-Awaisi, op. cit., pp. 35ff.

them taken to police stations." Nor were the Muslim Brothers viewed with favor in Sunni Islam's most important educational institution, the Al-Azhar mosque-university, whose rector, Mustafa al-Maragi, forbade his Palestinian students from indulging in any anti-Jewish propaganda.[48]

The partition plan for Palestine published by the British Peel Commission in July 1937 further fuelled the protest movement in Egypt. Not the least under the impact of the revolt that started in 1936 in Palestine, the Commission excluded the possibility of good relations between Arabs and Jews in a common state. According to its plan, the Jewish state would comprise the coastal strips and Galilee, covering less than a fourth of the territory, while the Arab state would include the remaining area, with the option of subsequent unity with Transjordan. A British-controlled corridor from Tel Aviv to Jerusalem would divide the Jewish and Arab states and a military presence there would hinder possible attacks.

By the time this plan became known, "Palestine" had already become a staple of public debate in Egypt. Now the project for a Jewish mini-state unleashed all-party protests as well as meeting with reservations from the Egyptian government. However, the character of these misgivings had little in common with the Mufti and Brotherhood's anti-Jewish campaigns.

Thus, the Wafd-party-led government proposed a united Palestinian state based on mutual tolerance and regulated immigration for all. This position was later spelt out in more detail by Ali Mahir, King Farouk's most important advisor. With reference to his personal experience and the well-established Arab-Jewish harmony in Egypt, Mahir rejected an independent Jewish state in Palestine; however, he "appreciated and respected the Zionist ideal" and fully recognized "the perseverance and ability of the Jews" in Palestine. The Arabs were ready to offer them all possi-

---

48. El-Awaisi, op. cit., p. 40 and Krämer, op.cit., p. 297.

ble guarantees and good cooperation. The prerequisite however was that the Zionist ideal should be revised by the limitation or cessation of Jewish immigration.[49]

The Muslim Brothers' campaign struck a different note. "On violent student demonstrations in Cairo, Alexandria and Tanta in April and May 1938 calls such as "down with the Jews", "Jews out of Egypt and Palestine" rang out.... Leaflets reiterated calls for a boycott of Jewish shops and businesses."[50] At the same time its newspaper, *al-Nadhir*, ran a regular column with the title "the Threat of the Jews in Egypt" in which the names and addresses of Jewish business proprietors and the owners of allegedly Jewish newspapers all over the world were published and all evil - from Communism to brothels - was attributed to the "Jewish threat."[51]

An appeal was made to young Egyptians to wear and consume only Islamic products and to prepare themselves in all parts of Egypt for jihad in defence of the Al-Aqsa mosque. *Al-Nadhir* called on children to give up their presents "for Palestine", while their mothers were to sacrifice their very selves. "I shall carry my life in my own hands and offer it as a sacrifice on the altar in defence of the Holy Place in order to win the honour of jihad" boasted one female fanatic in the paper. In 1939 the first bombs were placed in a Cairo synagogue and Jewish private homes.[52]

These anti-Jewish excesses were by then supported by other Islamist organizations such as the Young Men's Muslim Association (YMMA). "However," wrote Gershoni and Jankowski, "the involvement of the Muslim Brotherhood in the issue was more

49.   This statement by Mahir at the London St James Conference (February 7 to March 14, 1939) is the clearest expression of the official Egyptian standpoint of the time, according to Gershoni and Jankowski, op. cit., pp. 187ff and 177.
50.   Krämer, op. cit., p. 292.
51.   El-Awaisi, op. cit., pp. 70ff.
52.   Krämer, op. cit., p. 295.

intense, and penetrated deeper into the fabric of Egyptian society, than that of the YMMA."[53]

Giselher Wirsing, a prominent journalist of the Third Reich and member of the SS, enthusiastically reported on the shockwaves that the "political earthquake centre" in Palestine had created in Egypt. He noted with satisfaction "a marked return to the religious traditions of Islam" and "a fierce hostility to Western liberalism. ... Recent developments in Egypt ... show how strongly this theocracy is able to revive itself after the first onrush of liberalism."[54]

This burgeoning Islamist movement was subsidized with German funds. As Brynjar Lia recounts in his monograph on the Muslim Brotherhood: "Documents seized in the flat of Wilhelm Stellbogen, the Director of the German News Agency (Deutsches Nachrichtenbüro) affiliated to the German Legation in Cairo, show that prior to October 1939 the Muslim Brothers received subsidies from this organization. Stellbogen was instrumental in transferring these funds, which were considerably larger than the subsidies offered to other anti-British activists, to the Brothers."[55]

These contributions enabled the Muslim Brotherhood to set up a printing plant with twenty-four employees and use the most up-to-date propaganda methods. For example, an eighty-page pamphlet called "Fire and Destruction in Palestine" with fifty photos of alleged acts of violence and torture was produced

---

53. Gershoni and Jankowski, op. cit., p. 180.
54. Giselher Wirsing, *Engländer, Juden, Araber in Palästina*, fifth revised edition (Leipzig: Eugen Diederichs Verlag, 1942), pp. 136ff. Wirsing visited Egypt and Palestine in 1936 and 1939 on behalf of the SS.
55. Brynjar Lia, *The Society of the Muslim Brothers in Egypt* (Reading: Ithaca Press, 1988), p. 175. The British secret service officer Seth Arsenian confirms this information: "Nazi agents also paid subversive groups, such as.... the *Ikhwan al-Muslimun* in Egypt, to run propaganda against the British in Palestine." See Seth Arsenian, "Wartime Propaganda in the Middle East," *Middle East Journal*, Vol. 2, No. 4 (1948), p. 425.

and several tens of thousands of copies distributed among the populace.

This first Islamist mass mobilization was a success. While in 1938 the majority of the Egyptian press had still refused to participate in an anti-Jewish campaign, by the end of the decade public concern about Palestine had been profoundly aroused and the Egyptian government's readiness to take an anti-Zionist line had hugely increased.[56]

This became apparent in October 1938 on the occasion of a "Parliamentary Conference for Arab and Muslim Countries" in support of Palestine held in Cairo. It was the Brotherhood that, in secret talks with the Saudi prince Faisal and the Imam of Kuwait, had initiated this conference and ensured its smooth running. Al-Banna's cohorts provided the stewarding, received the delegations, ensured the separation of men and women and organized the distribution of antisemitic tracts, including the Arabic versions of *Mein Kampf* and the *Protocols of the Elders of Zion*.[57]

What was decisive, however, was that the Egyptian government decided to take part in the conference. The Muslim Brothers could consider the fact that the Egyptian Prime Minister, Muhammad Mahmud, not only held a banquet, but for the first time also made a pro-Palestinian speech the greatest success of their campaign to date. We will return to this conference and the impression it made in London later. Before we get to that, another question demands our attention: that of the role of the Nazi regime in influencing events in Egypt and Palestine.

The Muslim Brothers, the Mufti and the Nazis
Throughout the Arab world, National Socialism often met with sympathy and not infrequently with enthusiasm. "We were racists, admiring Nazism, reading its books and the source of its thought, particularly Nietzsche, Fichte, and H. S. Chamberlain,"

56. Krämer, op. cit., pp. 290 and 298.
57. El-Awaisi, op. cit., pp. 81ff and Krämer, op. cit., p. 295.

wrote Sami al-Jundi, a leader of the Syrian Baath Party, about the mood of many Arabs in the 1930s. "We were the first to think of translating *Mein Kampf*. Whoever lived during this period in Damascus would appreciate the inclination of the Arab people to Nazism, for Nazism was the power which could serve as its champion."[58] This affinity was not only based on the conviction they were fighting the same enemies - Britain and France. In addition, the German idea of the people (*"Volk,"*) defined by language, culture and blood rather than borders and political sovereignty, was far closer to the Islamic notion of the *umma* than to the British or French concept of citizenship. For in the Arab as well as German tradition, communities, not individuals, are the basic element.[59]

Back in 1932 Antun Saadeh had founded the Syrian People's Party which asserted the superiority of Syrians over other peoples and followed Nazi models even in its outward expressions - a swastika-like flag, the open-handed salute, etc.[60] On January 30, 1933 a German diplomat reported from the Lebanese capital Beirut on the "enthusiasm of broad circles for the national socialist awakening of Germany." Here, in 1936, the *Phalanges Libanaises* (with reference to the Spanish *Falange*), also organized according to the leadership principle, were founded.[61] In 1935 the Iraqi government established an official youth organization called *Futuwwa* whose task, according to the Iraqi Prime

58. Itamar Rabinovich, "Germany and the Syrian Political Scene in the late 1930s," in Jehuda L. Wallach (ed.), *Germany and the Middle East 1835-1939*, (International Symposium of the University of Tel Aviv: Nateev-Press, April 1975), pp. 194-5.
59. Bernard Lewis, *Semites and Anti-Semites* (London: Weidenfeld and Nicolson, 1986) p. 145; Bassam Tibi, *Der Islam und Deutschland. Muslime in Deutschland* (Stuttgart: Deutsche Verlags-Anstalt, 2000b), pp. 158ff.
60. Tibi, 2000b op. cit., pp. 158ff. The Syrian People's Party, according to Lewis, op. cit., p. 148, is also known as the Syrian National Socialist Party (later changed to Social-Nationalist Party).
61. Fueß, op. cit., p. 125; Fritz Steppat, "Das Jahr 1933 und seine Folgen für die arabischen Länder des Vorderen Orients" in Gerhard Schulz (ed.) *Die Große Krise der dreißiger Jahre. Vom Niedergang der Weltwirtschaft zum Zweiten Weltkrieg* (Göttingen: Vandenhoeck & Ruprecht, 1985), pp. 273ff.

Minister, was to educate "Iraqi youth in the military spirit in the German fashion" and sent a delegation to march with the Hitler Youth at the 1938 Nuremberg Nazi party rally. Finally in 1933, in Egypt Ahmad Husayn created the "Young Egypt" movement with some 2,000 members, which he drilled in paramilitary fashion with fascist salutes, torchlight processions and a leadership cult. A delegation of these "Green Shirts" took part in the 1936 Nuremberg Nazi party rally. Husayn's rabid antisemitism led him to hold the Jews responsible for "cultural squalor" and "filthy arts." "They are the secret of religious and moral decay," he declared in 1939, "to the point where it has become correct to say 'search for the Jew behind every depravity.'"[62]

The relationship between the Muslim Brothers and the Nazis has received less attention. Their distribution of *Mein Kampf* was not the only occasion when the Muslim Brothers stood with the Nazis. Thus al-Banna collaborated with the Third Reich's Egyptian agents and at the start of 1941 conferred with the leadership of Young Egypt over a plan to launch an anti-British uprising in Egypt to support the German war effort against Britain.[63] The Brotherhood's paramilitary wing offered the Nazis their support with not just a few of these activists being recruited by the German secret services.[64] However, it would be wrong to characterize the Muslim Brothers as ardent followers of the Nazis. The Brotherhood rejected the Nazis' race policies and German supremacist nationalism, since both were at odds with their concept of the *umma* as the universal Islamic brotherhood. Moreover, al-Banna was far too religious a man to accept a non-Muslim leader such

---

62. Robert Wistrich, *Hitler's Apocalypse, Jews and the Nazi Legacy*, London: Weidenfeld & Nicolson, 1985, p. 172. Husayn's admiration for the Nazis came to a swift end with the German entry into Prague. Thereafter he condemned the Axis powers for their aggression against small nations. Nonetheless, the ideology of the Young Egypt movement continued to bear the stamp of National Socialism. See Gershoni/Jankowski, op. cit., p. 15.
63. El-Awaisi, op. cit., p. 111.
64. Martin A. Lee, *The Swastika and the Crescent, Intelligence Report 2002*, p. 2. No systematic study of the mutual relationship is currently available.

as Hitler as his model.[65] When they did express admiration of certain aspects of Nazism, it was usually in the context of demonstrating that the Europeans had implemented some of 'the principles of Islam', such as a modest dress code, encouragement of early marriage, a strong patriotism and a military jihad spirit, rather than the other way around.[66]

The situation was different in the case of Amin al-Husseini, who had held the office of Mufti of Jerusalem since 1921. Even if in the 1930s some Arab nationalists saw Germany as an ally against the British without taking a great interest in the nature of the Hitler regime, the Mufti knew what that nature was and was attracted by it for that very reason.

As early as spring 1933, he assured the German consul in Jerusalem that "the Muslims inside and outside Palestine welcomed the new regime of Germany and hoped for the extension of the fascist, anti-democratic governmental system to other countries."[67] The youth organization of the party established by the Mufti operated for a time under the name Nazi Scouts. It adopted Hitler Youth-style shorts and leather belts and distributed leaflets emblazoned with Nazi slogans and swastikas.[68] When Hitler promulgated the Nuremberg race laws in 1935, he received telegrams of congratulation from throughout the Arab and Islamic worlds, but in particular "from Palestine, where German propaganda had been most active."[69]

The Nazis had very early on adopted an anti-Zionist stance. In 1921 Arthur Rosenberg, later to become the Nazis' chief propagandist, published a book entitled *Der staatsfeindliche*

---

65. Edmond Cao-Van-Hoa, *"Der Feind meines Feindes..." Darstellungen des nationalsozialistischen Deutschland in ägyptischen Schriften* (Frankfurt-am-Main: Peter Lang, 1990), p. 98.
66. Lia, op. cit., pp 80 and 180.
67. Yehuda Porath, *The Palestinian Arab National Movement. From Riots to Rebellion*, Vol. II, 1929-1939 (London: Frank Cass, 1977), p. 76.
68. Lionel van der Meulen, *Fremde im eigenen Land. Die Geschichte der Palästinenser und der PLO* (Munich: Knesebeck & Schuler, 1989), p. 77.
69. Lewis, op. cit., p. 176.

Zionismus ("Zionism, Enemy of the State.") "In Palestine," wrote Rosenberg, "the Jews are using the old method of exploiting and driving out by legal means the real population which has lived here for thousands of years in order to create a purely Jewish... gathering point for pursuing a wide-ranging oriental policy." Since "the Jew" can never be "truly creative," it would be quite wrong to talk about a "state," according to Rosenberg.[70] In 1925, Hitler developed this thought further in *Mein Kampf*: the Jews "do not at all intend to build a Jewish state in Palestine... They only want an organization centre for their international world-swindling furnished with its own state rights and free from the reach of other states, a place of refuge for convicted scoundrels and a university for up-and-coming swindlers."[71] Does not this phraseology already express the sense of later anti-Zionist terms of abuse such as "entity" and "settler regime?" Nonetheless, until 1937 the Nazis did not adopt an openly anti-Zionist policy. As long as the Germans still retained a glimmer of hope that they could remain on good terms with the British, they diligently avoided any blatantly anti-British acts.

In the summer of 1937, however, a new situation arose due to the Peel Commission's partition plan, which included the creation of a Jewish state. German Foreign Minister von Neurath emphasized in a memorandum that "the creation of a Jewish state" was not "in Germany's interest" since such a state "would create an additional position of power under international law for international Jewry. Germany therefore has an interest in strengthening the Arab world as a counterweight against such a possible increase in power for world Jewry."[72]

Strengthening the Arabs against the Jews – it is true that Berlin initially pursued this new course surreptitiously. However,

70. Alfred Rosenberg, *Der staatsfeindliche Zionismus,* citations from the 1938 Munich edition (Zentralverlag der NSDAP, Munich, 1938), pp. 85-87.
71. Adolf Hitler, *Mein Kampf* (Vol. II – Munich: Verlag Franz Eher Nachfolger, 1925), p. 356.
72. Lewis, op. cit., p. 170.

the scale of the operations now set in motion was nonetheless impressive. Students from Arab countries received German scholarships, firms took on Arab apprentices, and Arab party leaders were invited to the Nuremberg party rallies and military chiefs to Wehrmacht manoeuvres. An "Arab Club" was established in Berlin as the centre for Palestine-related agitation and Arabic-language broadcasting.[73]

Under the direction of the German Propaganda Ministry, the Deutsches Nachrichtenbüro (German News Agency - DNB), whose regional headquarters in Jerusalem had set up an Arab service in 1936, stepped up its work. The head of DNB-Jerusalem, Dr Franz Reichert, who had excellent links not only with the Mufti, but also with the Arabic press, bribed journalists and brought dissident newspapers back on board with lucrative advertising orders.

In September 1937, two members of the Jewish Department of the SS' secret service, (Sicherheitsdienst - SD), including Adolf Eichmann, carried out an exploratory mission in the Middle East lasting several weeks. Extended visits by the leader of the Hitler Youth, Baldur von Schirach, and the head of the Abwehr (counter-intelligence service), Wilhelm Canaris, followed. Finally, in April 1939, the head of the Foreign Office's Oriental Department, Otto von Hentig, also spent time in Palestine and Egypt. This activism was not without results: von Schirach donated the money for the establishment of an "Arab Club" in Damascus in which German Nazis trained recruits for the Mufti's insurgents and Canaris covered the region with a spy network.[74]

---

73. Robert Melka, *The Axis and the Arab Middle East 1930-1945*, (thesis, University of Minnesota, University Micro-films, Inc., Ann Arbor, MI, 1966), p. 53. On the Arabic-language short wave transmitter based in Zeesen see: Matthias Küntzel, "National Socialism and Antisemitism in the Arab World," *Jewish Political Studies Review*, Spring 2005, Vol. 17, No. 1 & 2, pp. 99-118.
74. J. C. Hurewitz, *The Struggle for Palestine* (New York: Norton, 1951), p. 87; Ralf Balke, *Die Landesgruppe der NSDAP in Palästina*, thesis, (Universität-Gesamthochschule Essen, 1997), p. 204; Melka op. cit., pp. 48ff; Michael Cohen, *Retreat from the Mandate* (New York, 1978), p. 58; Lukasz Hirszowicz,

Now the Mufti's tirelessly reiterated appeals for cooperation were heeded and answered in the form of supplies of money
and weapons. In 1937-39, the ability to sustain the "Arab revolt"
depended not the least on Berlin. "The Mufti himself," wrote
Klaus Gensicke in his seminal study, "acknowledged that at that
time it was only due to the German funds he received that it had
been possible to carry through the uprising in Palestine. From
the outset, he made high financial demands which the Nazis to
a great extent met."[75] In addition, German weapons were sent
through secret channels to the insurgents. Admiral Canaris,
head of German military intelligence, later revealed that shortly
before the start of the war he met with the Mufti's secretary "several times in order personally to discuss the issue of transporting
weapons to the Arab insurgents," weapons intended primarily
for killing off the Jewish homeland in Palestine.[76]

The Mufti's Antisemitism
The Mufti's father had already fought against Jewish immigrants
in Palestine back in the days of the Ottomans. In the First World
War as a soldier in the Ottoman armies, Amin el-Husseini had
developed an admiration for German military discipline com-
monplace there. In 1920, soon after his return to the mandate
territory, he incited anti-Jewish riots in Jerusalem, which led for
the first time to deaths and many injured.[77] His antisemitism had
taken shape before the Nazis gained power. This was particularly evident in August 1929, during a Mufti-inspired pogrom in
Jerusalem that was directed not against Zionists, but Jews - the
victims belonging to the centuries-old communities of Safed and

The Third Reich and the Arab East (London: Routledge & Kegan Paul, 1966),
p. 54.
75. Klaus Gensicke, Der Mufti von Jerusalem Amin el-Husseini und die Nationalsozialisten (Frankfurt-am-Main: Peter Lang, 1988), p. 234.
76. Gensicke, op. cit., p. 94.
77. Taysir Jbara, Palestinian Leader Hajj Amin al-Husayni, Mufti of Jerusalem
(Princeton: Kingston Press, 1985), pp. 32ff and Krämer 2002, pp. 245ff.

Hebron. The riots spread throughout Palestine; in Hebron alone more than sixty Jews were butchered. It took six days for British and Zionist troops to stop the pogrom, which cost the lives of 133 Jews and 116 Arabs. "The riots of 1929 marked a turning-point in Arab-Jewish relations in Palestine," concluded Walter Laqueur.[78]

In fact, nobody had a more decisive influence on the early history of the Middle Eastern conflict than the Mufti, who as President of the Muslim Supreme Council was the highest religious authority. El-Husseini tirelessly used this religious office to Islamise anti-Zionism and provide a religious rationale for the hatred of Jews. Anyone who failed to accept his guidelines would be denounced by name in the mosque during Friday prayers, excluded from rites of marriage and burial, or physically threatened.[79] In declaring this anti-Jewish struggle a religious duty, the Mufti placed the Palestine conflict in a pan-Islamic context: his hatred of the Jews was also a declaration of war on the "invasion of liberal ideas" into the world of Islam.

The Mufti hated Western civilization, which the Zionists were introducing into Palestine, with undisguised passion.[80] His primary aim was to combat such achievements of modernity as freedom of thought, women's equality and secularism. Speaking at a religious conference in 1935, the Mufti complained: "The cinema, the theatre and some shameless magazines enter our houses

---

78. Walter Laqueur, *A History of Zionism* (New York: Schocken Books, 1972), p. 256. Lionel van der Meulen, op. cit., p. 67; Mordechai Naor, *Eretz Israel. Das 20. Jahrhundert* (Cologne: Könemann, 1998), p. 156.
79. David Th. Schiller, *Palästinenser zwischen Terrorismus und Diplomatie. Die paramilitärische palästinensische Nationalbewegung won 1918 bis 1981* (Munich: Bernard & Graefe, 1982) op. cit., p 146; Nels Johnson, *Islam and the Politics of Meaning in Palestinian Nationalism* (London: Kegan Paul International, 1982), pp. 51ff.
80. "He hates Western civilization with undisguised passion," reported American journalist David W. Nussbaum after having visited the Mufti in 1946, "and except when he fled to Germany, had always given it a wide berth." Cited in: Joseph B. Schechtman, The Mufti and the Fuehrer, New York: Thomas Yoseloff, 1965, p. 289.

and courtyards like adders, where they kill morality and demolish the foundation of society." The Jews were blamed for this alleged corruption of moral values, as demonstrated by another statement of Amin el-Husseini: "They [i.e. the Jews] have also spread here their customs and usages which are opposed to our religion and to our whole way of life. The Jewish girls who run around in shorts demoralise our youth by their mere presence."[81]

However, there were many Muslims at that time who did not feel threatened by these changes at all. The century-long history of Islamic modernism began at the start of the nineteenth century, reaching full bloom between 1860 and 1930. For example, in 1839 the Ottoman Sultan decreed equality for Jews and Christians and in 1856 this equality was established in law. This measure was motivated not only by pressure from the European colonial powers, but also by the desire of the Ottoman elite to draw closer to European civilization. Of course the discriminatory dhimmi status decreed for Jews and Christians by traditional Islam did not vanish immediately or everywhere.

Some Jewish communities in several Arab lands, especially in North Africa and Iran still suffered severe humiliations.[82] But at least in the urban centres, Jews were permitted to become members of Parliament, hold government posts and, after 1909, were recruited into the military.[83]

In the 1920s the bulk of the Islamic elites no longer lived under sharia law. Kemal Atatürk's regime abolished it in Turkey in 1924. In 1925 Iran began to secularize under Reza Shah. In Egypt, sharia law only applied in the personal sphere, otherwise the legal code was of European provenance.[84] In this period rather

81. Uri M. Kupferschmidt, *The Supreme Muslim Council. Islam under the British Mandate for Palestine* (Leiden: E. J. Brill, 1987), pp. 249ff and 252.
82. Bat Ye'or, *Islam and Dhimmitude. Where Civilizations Collide*, (Cranbury, NJ: Associated University Presses, 2002), pp. 123-173.
83. Yossef Bodanski, Islamic Antisemitism as a Political Instrument, Shaarei Tikva (The Ariel Center for Policy Research) 1999, S. 20-25.
84. Albert Hourani, Die Geschichte der arabischen Völker, Frankfurt/M. (Fischer Taschenbuch), 2000, S. 420.

than the nation being a sub-unit of Islam, Islam was a sub-unit of the nation, in which Muslims, Christians and Jews enjoyed equal rights.[85]

To Islamic traditionalists this advance of modernity was an outrage. Their resistance laid the groundwork for the Islamist movement which was from the outset both anti-modern and anti-Jewish. Its three leading protagonists were Amin el-Husseini, Hassan al-Banna and Izz al-Din al-Qassam, who lived in Haifa and in 1935 died a martyr's death as the twentieth century's first Islamist. Their common teacher was Rashid Rida, a religious scholar heavily influenced by the Saudi Wahhabites. Rida's three prominent students followed their master in demanding a return to sharia law and traditional Islam, in order to drive Western civilization from Palestine and the Arab world, before going on to defeat it throughout the world. They saw Jerusalem as the crystallization point for the "rebirth of Islam" and Palestine as the centre from whence resistance to the Jews and the modern world was destined to emanate.

Later, in the course of the Second World War Amin el-Husseini developed into by far the most committed supporter of National Socialism in the Arab and Islamic world. After instigating a pro-German putsch in Baghdad in 1941 he reached Berlin from where, with a staff of sixty Arabs, he sought to serve the causes of National Socialism and the Islamic world.[86]

He summarized what he considered the most important intersections between Islam and National Socialism as follows:

1. Monotheism - unity of leadership, the leadership principle;
2. A sense of obedience and discipline;
3. The battle and the honour of dying in battle;

---

85. Lewis, Semites and Anti-Semites, S. 136.
86. 180 Jews in Baghdad lost their lives in this putsch attempt. See Hayyim J. Cohen, "The Anti-Jewish Farhud in Baghdad, 1941," *Middle Eastern Studies*, Vol. 3, October 1966, No. 1, pp. 2-17.

4. Community, following the principle: the collective before the individual;

5. High esteem for motherhood and prohibition of abortion;

6. Glorification of work and creativity: "Islam protects and values productive work, of whatever kind it may be;"

7. Attitude towards the Jews - "in the struggle against Jewry, Islam and National Socialism are very close."[87]

As regards antisemitism, the Mufti easily matched the Germans in the field of conspiracy theories. In 1942 he declared on the occasion of the landing of American troops in North Africa that, "the Americans are the willing slaves of the Jews" and "as such the enemies of Islam and the Arabs."[88]

His most effective propaganda tool was the Arabic-language broadcasting out of Zeesen, a town with some four thousand inhabitants to the south of Berlin. From 1939 onward, Zeesen broadcast its daily Arabic-language program. Of all the foreign-language services, the Oriental Service had "absolute priority. It reached out to Arabs, Turks, Persians, and Indians and had an eighty-strong staff, including freelance announcers and translators."[89] Between 1939 and 1945, at a time when, in the Arab world, listening to the radio took place primarily in public squares or bazaars and coffee houses, no other station was more popular than the Zeesen service, which skillfully mingled antisemitic propaganda with quotations from the Koran and Arabic music. From 1941 onward the Mufti lived in Berlin, supervising Arabic radio broadcasting out of Zeesen.

The Mufti also agreed with the Nazis regarding what should happen to the Jews. In his 1940 draft for German-Italian state-

87. Talk by the Mufti for the Imams of the Bosnian SS-Division on October 4, 1944, cited in Gerhard Höpp (ed.), *Mufti-Papiere. Briefe, Memoranden, Reden und Aufrufe Amin al-Husainis aus dem Exil 1940-1945* (Berlin, Klaus Schwarz, 2001), pp. 219ff.
88. Gensicke, op. cit., p. 120.
89. Werner Schwipps, "Wortschlacht im Äther," in Deutsche Welle, ed., *Wortschlacht im Äther. Der deutsche Auslandsrundfunk im Zweiten Weltkrieg* (Berlin: Haude & Spenersche Verlagsbuchhandlung, 1971), p. 58.

statement we read, "Germany and Italy recognise the right of the Arab countries to resolve the question of the Jewish elements … in the same way as the Jewish question has been resolved in Germany and Italy."[90] Indeed, since summer 1942 an SS special unit had been on standby in Athens, ready to implement the Shoah in Palestine in alliance with the Nazis' Arab allies following an anticipated victory by Rommel in the North African theatre.[91]

The Mufti only ever criticized Nazi policy when he feared that Jews might escape the Holocaust. He was on friendly terms with Heinrich Himmler, whom he admired. Their friendship was, however, strained when in 1943 Himmler wanted (as a propaganda stunt and in return for the release of 20,000 German prisoners) to permit 5,000 Jewish children to emigrate - and therefore survive. The Mufti, who, according to a German government official, "would prefer all of them (the Jews) to be killed," fought tirelessly against this plan. With success! The children were dispatched to the gas chambers.[92] The Mufti showed special interest in reacting to decisions by the governments of Bulgaria, Romania and Hungary to allow some thousands of Jewish children accompanied by responsible adults to leave for Palestine. It would be "appropriate and more expedient" he wrote promptly to the Bulgarian Foreign Minister, "to prevent the Jews from emigrating from your country and send them somewhere where they will be under strict control, for example to Poland." Another success! Already issued emigration permits were withdrawn and the salvation of the Jewish children prevented.[93]

90. The verbatim text of the draft can be found in Fritz Grobba, *Männer und Mächte im Orient* (Göttingen: Musterschmidt, 1967) pp. 197ff.
91. The existence of this unit was first revealed in 2006. See the excellent study by Klaus-Michael Mallmann/Martin Cüppers, *Halbmond und Hakenkreuz. Das Dritte Reich, die Araber und Palästina* (Darmstadt: Wissenschaftliche Buchgesellschaft, 2006), pp. 137-47.
92. Gensicke, op. cit., p. 156.
93. Höpp (ed.), op. cit., pp. 149ff and Simon Wiesenthal, *Großmufti – Großagent der Achse* (Salzburg-Wien: Ried-Verlag, 1947), pp. 42ff.

In the course of constant round-trips the Mufti strove to ensure that "the Palestine question unites all Arab countries in common hatred of Britain and the Jews" as he wrote proudly to Hitler in 1941.[94] To this end he worked especially closely with the Muslim Brothers. Al-Banna had made contact with el-Husseini back in 1927, a year before the founding of the Brotherhood.[95] Twenty years later the Mufti, despite his record of collaboration with the Nazis, was appointed leader of the Brotherhood in Palestine and al-Banna's deputy. El-Husseini's opinion of the Brotherhood was no less high. "I believe in the Muslim Brothers as they are the troops of God who shall defeat the troops of Satan," he declared in 1946.[96]

As we shall see, the alliance between al-Banna and el-Husseini had disastrous consequences for both the Jews and Arabs of Palestine leading up to the establishment of the state of Israel. The significance of their cooperation, however, will only become plain if we refocus our attention on the situation in Palestine.

Nashashibis versus Husseinis

In Palestine, the contradictions between non-Jewish Arabs and non-Arab Jews followed far less clear lines than was often later claimed. At the turn of the century it was primarily the Christian Arabs who, under the influence of French and Jesuit antisemites, raged against the Jews in their newspapers.[97] Although the majority of Palestine Arabs rejected the Balfour Declaration in March and April 1920 many village sheikhs in Judea and Galilee distanced themselves from the wave of anti-Zionism passing through the towns of Palestine at that time and signed petitions supporting Jewish immigration to the country.[98]

---

94. Höpp (ed.), op. cit., p. 21.
95. El-Awaisi, op. cit., p. 28.
96. El-Awaisi, op. cit., p. 191.
97. Laqueur, op. cit. p. 212.
98. David Th. Schiller op. cit. pp 91ff.

Hillel Cohen's pioneering study *Palestinian Collaboration With Zionism 1917-1948* enumerates the motives for Palestinian Arabs to cooperate with Zionists. Some promised themselves personal gain - supplementary income or employment - others co-operated in what they considered to be the best interest of their tribes villages or nation while the motivations of a third group "were ethical and humanist: they had Jews as friends and neighbors and were digusted by the violence of the Palestinian national movement." [99]

Of the 970,000 people living in the British mandate territory in 1931, 70% were Muslims, 10% Christians and some 20% native Arab or immigrant Jews. [100] The Muslims were over-represented in the rural areas, while the overwhelming majority of the Christian Arabs lived in the towns, belonging almost exclusively to the upper middle classes - lawyers, doctors, journalists, etc. This distribution reflected the level of literacy: 70% of Christians, but only 25% of Muslims could read. The ruling class of Palestinian Arab society consisted of figures from the major landowning families such as the Husseinis, Nashashibis, Khalidis or Daganis, known as "effendis." The notables of the Palestinian towns were closely bound to and dependent on this elite and its local outcrops. [101] This segmentation of the Palestinian population, both vertically and horizontally into clans, decisively shaped the course of the confrontation with Zionism.

Thus the bitter conflict between the two most influential clans, the Nashashibis and the Husseinis, mainly expressed itself in the form of different attitudes to the Jewish immigrants and the British mandate authorities. The Nashashibis also wanted to restrict Jewish immigration and prevent Zionist dominance over

99. Hillel Cohen, *Army of Shadows. Palestinian Collaboration With Zionism 1917-1948*, manuscript p. 73. This book is forthcoming from University of California Press in winter 2007.
100. Hermann Meier-Cronemeyer, *Geschichte des Staates Israel, Vol 1* (Schwalbach/Ts.: Wochenschau-Verlag, 1997), p. 106.
101. David Th. Schiller, op. cit., pp. 92ff.

Arabs. However, in all phases of the conflict they advocated a moderate policy towards the Zionists and British and supported limited cooperation with both groups. Thus, as Mayor of Jerusalem since 1927, Rashib Nashashibi worked with a Jewish and a Christian deputy.[102] "Towards the end of the 1920s the notables in the towns and cities sided with the Nashashibis," writes Lionel van der Meulen, "to this group, over a third of whom were Christians, the Husseinis' emphatically Islamic line was alarming. They feared that they would lose more freedom and influence under the Mufti than under the leadership of the more secular and Arab nationalist-inclined Nashashibis."[103]

In contrast to the Husseinis, in 1936 the Nashashibis advocated collaboration with the British Peel Commission, which was considering the mandate territory's future. Alongside the Regent of Transjordan, Abdullah, in 1937 the Nashashibi clan supported the division of Palestine into two independent states as recommended by the Peel Commission. While the World Zionist Congress also accepted the plan, el-Husseini rejected any Jewish state in Palestine: the first two-state project for Palestine was thwarted mainly by his intransigence.[104]

The power struggle between the Husseinis and Nashashibis culminated during the disturbances of 1936-39. Since the rate of Jewish immigration had risen abruptly as a result of the Nazi regime in Germany - from about 4,000 in 1931 to 60,000 in 1935 - in 1936 the non-Jewish Arabs under the Mufti's leadership launched a general strike in support of a total end to immigration, a ban on the sale of land to Jews and the establishment of a Palestinian representative authority. When the strike began to flag in the summer, various guerrilla groups came to the forefront, especially in rural areas. Gradually, the strike was replaced by a kind of institutionalized banditry. Not all of these bandits, of course,

---

102. Naor, op. cit., p. 144.
103. Lionel van der Meulen, op. cit., p. 67.
104. David Th. Schiller, op. cit., pp. 138ff.

appeared on the scene without direction: "The Mufti consciously eliminated his opponents within the Palestinian camp with the utmost brutality," writes Abraham Ashkenasi. "The Palestinian revolt of 1936-39 was also an assault on the Mufti's opponents. There were more murders and homicides inside the Palestinian camp than were perpetrated against the Jews or British."[105]

In fact, in the areas controlled by the Mufti's gangs, new dress codes and *sharia* courts were brutally enforced and numerous "un-Islamic" deviationists liquidated on a vast scale with unprecedented violence. Alongside the Jews and the British, Palestinians who sought compromises with Zionism and the Mandatory power and supported the Peel Plan were also targeted. "Sellers of land to the Jews, holders of moderate political views and those whose nationalism was generally suspected," reports Porath, "were not always immediately murdered; sometimes they were kidnapped and taken to the mountainous areas under rebel control. There they were thrown into pits infested with snakes and scorpions. After spending a few days there, the victims, if still alive, were brought before one of the rebel courts and usually sentenced to death, or, as a special dispensation, to severe flogging. The terror was so strong that no one, including *ulama* and priests, dared to perform the proper burial services."[106]

The effect of these practices was that ever wider sections of the population denounced the "insurgents" to the British and armed themselves against attacks by the Mufti's gangs. By autumn 1938 the "open opposition of parts of the Arab population to the Mufti's policy" could no longer be overlooked, reports David Th. Schiller. "This opposition began to form under the leadership of the Nashashibis."[107] The effect of these years on Arab society was disastrous. Any prospect of the development of a modern soci-

105. According to Abraham Ashkenasi in his preface to Gensicke's study, op. cit., p. 7.
106. Porath, op. cit., p. 250.
107. David Th. Schiller, op. cit., pp. 163 and 138ff.

ety was abruptly ended. "The Arab community broke free from the rule of law, disengaged from the British mandatory power's legal system and dispensed arbitrary justice through unbridled violence... The last shreds of pluralism and free debate vanished and were replaced by blackmail and intimidation, censorship and intellectual terrorism." [108]

In 1938 the British mandate power began more firmly to suppress the "revolt," inspiring a torrent of abuse from the Nazi paper *Der völkische Beobachter* about British brutality against the Palestinian "freedom-fighters." The financial and military backing provided by Nazi Germany to the Mufti's side in this war brings home the fact that this was a kind of preliminary skirmish between the opponents in the Second World War.

A biography of the Mufti published in Berlin in 1943 makes plain the ideological affinities between National Socialism and Islamism from the German point of view. The very existence of this book is in itself remarkable, since it shows that not only was the Mufti enamoured of the Germans, but that Germans reciprocated the sentiment. Still more instructive, however, is the admiration the author displays for the efforts of the Mufti's gangs to impose Islamic social conformity in the 1937-39 period. The following document illustrates what "liberation struggle" meant for the German and Arab movements:

"In a tree-lined street in Jerusalem's Old Town the police find two Arabs lying face-downwards, clearly struck down by bullets through the back, the entry wounds carefully covered with the headgear known in Europe as the 'fez' and in the East as the 'tarbush.' One of the dead is a well-known lawyer, the other a prosperous landlord.... Both are Arabs, shot by fellow Arabs. Their crime was to have ignored the recent instruction from the insurgent General, which had been posted on every corner in Jerusalem, 'In the name of Allah the Beneficent, the

108. Mallmann/Cüppers, op. cit., p. 36.

Merciful! The headquarters of the Arab revolution reminds all the Arabs of Palestine that the tarbush is not the true national headgear of the Arabs. The Arabs of Palestine must immediately remove their tarbushes, the garb of their former oppressors, and wear the national *kaffiyeh*. Those who, despite our warnings, persist in wearing the *tarbush*, will be considered our enemies. They will be dealt with in the same way as those who actively participate in fighting our glorious revolutionary army. Signed: the leader of the revolutionary Arabs'. Following this decree from the revolutionary leader, the tarbush disappeared from the streets of Palestinian towns and cities virtually from one day to the next. In similar vein, the country's women were forbidden to wear the European-style hats popular among the upper social strata, and with similar despatch Palestine's Arab women all returned to wearing the Arab headscarf. Thus did tarbushes and Paris-fashion hats vanish from the city streets, and with them the signs with which the educated or rich wished to distinguish themselves from the simple countryfolk."[109]

Almost as if describing a theatrical performance, the Nazi author here depicts exactly that model of a dictatorial-egalitarian utopia which the Muslim Brothers envisaged for Egypt: the annihilation of any individuality seeking to distance itself from the stifling collectivity. As we have already seen, the Brotherhood had used the unrest in Palestine to further its anti-Jewish and pro-Islamic campaigns. But it had also intervened in the struggles within the Palestinian camp: they considered the Nashashibis to be traitors, "separatists" and British agents. They not only prevented any Egyptian aid from reaching the Nashashibis, they also called on the Palestinian people to slay all members and supporters of the Nashashibis in Allah's name.[110] The Mufti's terror, on the other hand, was given total support and celebrated in

---

109. Kurt Fischer-Weth, *Amin al-Husseini. Großmufti von Palästina* (Berlin: Walter Tietz, 1943), pp. 82ff.
110. El-Awaisi, op. cit., p. 89.

Egypt as a signal for jihad. Not without success! In October 1938 in Cairo, the cooperation between al-Banna and el-Husseini led to the previously mentioned Parliamentary Conference for Arab and Islamic Countries, government support that effectively signalled a revision of Egyptian policy.

In London, where the priority leading up to the oncoming world war was the maintenance of good relations with the Arab world, the Egyptian convergence with the Islamic movement and the Islamization of the Palestine conflict were viewed with the utmost concern: on November 9,1938, as synagogues burned in Germany, the British government hit the panic button. Four weeks after the Cairo conference the Peel Commission's proposal for a division of Palestine, which had been accepted by the Jews and rejected by el-Husseini, was withdrawn, "since meanwhile the Arabs," writes Hermann Meier-Cronemeyer, "at an interparliamentary conference of Arab and Muslim countries for the defence of Palestine in October 1938 in Cairo had threatened to ally with the Axis Powers."[111]

It would be ten years before, in 1947, the United Nations would introduce a new partition plan. In the intervening period the Nazi annihilation of Europe's Jews ran its course.

The Sanctuary of National Socialism
On May 8 1945, the world gradually began to have a foreboding of the crimes that had been committed in Auschwitz, Treblinka and the other centres of industrial mass murder. Until 1945 the majority of Jews, not to mention non-Jews, had rejected Zionism as the wrong answer to antisemitism. Horrifically, only now in retrospect, had it been proved the only reasonable answer given the historical circumstances. Now, it was not only the United States that supported the creation of a Jewish state. On May 1947 the Soviet Foreign Minister Andrei Gromyko, also laid down

111. Meier-Cronemeyer, op. cit., p. 105.

the Soviet "Balfour Doctrine" in a speech to the United Nations. "Past experience, particularly during the Second World War, shows that no western European State was able to provide adequate assistance for the Jewish people in defending its rights and its very existence from the violence of the Hitlerites and their allies... [This] explains the aspirations of the Jews to establish their own State. It would be unjust not to take this into consideration and to deny the right of the Jewish people to realize this aspiration. It would be unjustifiable to deny this right to the Jewish people, particularly in view of all it has undergone during the Second World War."[112]

On November 26, 1947 Gromyko disagreed with the Arab view that the partition of Palestine was a historic injustice. "This view of the case is unacceptable, if only because, after all, the Jewish people has been closely linked with Palestine for a considerable period in history... [Moreover], it may not be amiss to remind my listeners again that, as a result of the war which was unleashed by Hitlerite Germany, the Jews, as a people, have suffered more than any other people."[113]

What, however, was the reaction in the Arab world and Egypt to the suffering of the Jewish people? What fate now awaited the Mufti of Jerusalem, who had been not only the most prominent leader of Arab Palestine, but also the Nazis' most sedulous ally in the Islamic world?

The Mufti left Berlin only in the dying days of the regime; as late as April 1945 he accepted 50,000 marks from the Foreign Office.[114] His flight to Switzerland led to his extradition to France where until 1946, with a chauffeur, two bodyguards and his Sec-

112. The United Nations General Assembly, Minutes of the 77th Plenary Meeting, May 14, 1947, at: http://www.mideastweb.org/gromyko1947.htm
113. The United Nations General Assembly, Minutes of the 125th Plenary Meeting, November 26, 1947, at: http://www.zionism-israel.com/zionism_ungromyko2.htm
114. Gensicke, op. cit., pp. 239 and 251. Gensicke describes in detail why el-Husseini was worth the money until the bitter end.

retary, he resided in the Villa Les Roses in the Parisian suburb of Louvecienne.

Yugoslavia had placed the Mufti on its war criminals list, since as organizer of the Muslim SS division on Bosnia-Herzegovina he had been responsible for the murder of thousands of Serbs and Croats.[115] Britain as well – though surprisingly unenthusiastic - asked the French government to hand over el-Husseini. As a result, the Muslim Brotherhood, which considered him to be the sole representative of Palestine, sent a telegram to the British ambassador in Cairo urging the latter to keep el-Husseini out of harm's way. Paris's refusal to extradite the Grand Mufti found an echo in the East too. The French ambassador in Cairo received numerous delegations wishing to thank the French government for its stance.[116]

When the United States supported Britain's application to have el-Husseini sentenced, Hassan al-Banna sent a protest memorandum to the American minister plenipotentiary which read: "We, in the name of the Muslim Brothers and all Arabs and Muslims, would like to warn your government not to continue this unjust Zionist policy. ...We would also like you to confirm to your government our preparedness to sacrifice ourselves for the sake of rescuing our men, whenever necessary."[117] After the Arab League had endorsed the Brotherhood's position, Britain, France and the United States gave way. Nobody wanted to fall out with the Arab world; Yugoslavia too finally yielded.[118]

Finally, the Mufti managed to leave France incognito. When on June 10, 1946 the headlines of the world press announced the

115. Gensicke, op. cit., p. 210.
116. Simon Wiesenthal, op. cit., p. 55.
117. This memo was published in: *Majallat al-Ikhwan al-Muslimun*, April 23, 1946. See: Al-Awaisi, op. cit., p. 188. The British hesitation is desribed by Josef B. Schechtman, *The Mufti and the Fuehrer* (New York – London: Thomas Yoseloff, 1965), pp. 168ff.
118. Philip Mattar, *The Mufti of Jerusalem. Al-Hajj Amin al-Husayni and the Palestinian National Movement* (New York: Columbia University Press, 1988), p. 109.

Mufti's "flight" from France, "the Arab quarters of Jerusalem and all the Arab towns and villages were garlanded and beflagged, and the great man's portrait was to be seen everywhere."[119] On June 19, 1946 King Farouk granted him asylum. The Egyptian government turned down a British extradition request referring to a ban on political activity imposed on the Mufti.[120] But the Mufti had absolutely no intention of restraining himself. As though he had not compromised himself in any way in Berlin, as Chairman of the Arab High Committee in Palestine he re-established his paramilitary youth organization, *al-Futuwwa*, and conferred with the Arab League aiming to ensure their total and eternal rejection of any partition plan for Palestine.[121]

When the Egyptian government began to talk about certain "political errors" made by the Mufti in his association with National Socialism, the Muslim Brothers were hot on their heels with a highly indignant repudiation. The Mufti, they declared, had made no mistakes; in Berlin he had been purely and simply carrying out jihad.[122]

Thus, the Muslim Brothers cleared the way for the second career of the Mufti, whose pro-Nazi past they considered a source of pride, not shame. Moreover, the lack of punishment for his commitment to Nazism only further increased the Mufti's prestige amongst Arabs. "In this impunity they see not only the weakness of the Europeans," Simon Wiesenthal wrote in 1947, "but absolution for past and future events. A man who can get away with anything, who is the Enemy number 1 of a powerful empire - and this empire cannot ward him off - definitely seems to them to be a suitable *Führer*."[123]

---

119. Daphne Trevor, *Under the White Paper* (Jerusalem: Jerusalem Press, 1948), pp. 206ff.
120. Jbara, op. cit., p. 186.
121. Mattar, op. cit., p. 108.
122. El-Awaisi, op. cit., p. 189.
123. Wiesenthal, op. cit., p. 2.

The Mufti was not of course the only Nazi drawn to Egypt. A large number of Nazi war criminals - estimated at several thousand - escaped justice through flight to Egypt. Why Egypt? On the one hand, pro-German feeling had grown especially strong there. When at the start of 1942 Rommel defeated the British armed forces and advanced towards Egypt, not only did a section of the Egyptian General Staff - including Gamal Abdel Nasser and Anwar as-Sadat - offer their support to the Germans; demonstrators hailed the field-marshal with calls of "Forward Rommel" and "We are Rommel's soldiers." A secret Zionist report of the time stated that 90% of Egyptian intellectuals and civil servants sympathized with the Axis.[124] Still more important was the fact that the acceptance of antisemitism had grown enormously in the preceding ten years, which meant that Nazi war criminals found more than just a hiding-place: "in Egypt they could continue their war against the Jews."[125]

In his analysis of a debate on Zionism and Nationalism broadcast on *Al-Jazeera* in May 2001, Götz Nordbruch concludes that in the Arab world "any viewpoint which calls into question the arguments of Holocaust-denial is branded as a betrayal of Palestinian and Arab rights," since, in the last analysis, according to Jordanian writer Ibrahim Alloush, "recognition of the Holocaust" lies at "the heart of cultural normalization with the Zionist enemy."[126]

The denial or even approval of the Shoah is the major reason for the schism that today divides the Arab intellectual world from the West.

The consequences of this historiographical gap are huge and play a decisive role in the Arab-Jewish conflict to this day. As long as it continues to deny the Shoah, Islamism can continue to

124. Krämer, op. cit., p. 307 and van der Meulen, op. cit., p. 95.
125. Lewis, op. cit., p. 160.
126. Götz Nordbruch, "Holocaustleugnung und Kampf gegen 'Normalisierung'. Arabische Diskussionen um den Holocaust" in *Der Rechte Rand*, nr. 72, Sept/Oct 2001, pp. 19ff.

explain international support for the establishment of Israel in 1947 in exclusively antisemitic terms, through conspiracy theories, as a Jewish-directed attack by the USA and the Soviet Union on the Arabs. Recognition of historical reality, on the other hand, would necessarily entail drawing the same conclusions as Andrei Gromyko did in 1947.

Thus, when the decision to partition Palestine was taken by the General Assembly on November 29, 1947, Hassan al-Banna considered "the whole United Nations intervention to be an international plot carried out by the Americans, the Russians and the British, under the influence of Zionism."[127] Accordingly, all the more uncompromisingly was the anti-Jewish holy war pursued simultaneously in three arenas - the villages of Palestine, the cities of Egypt and the headquarters of the United Nations. "So why hesitate, why hold back when the breeze of paradise is blowing and carries the scent of martyrdom?" declared al-Banna.[128]

War against Israel

In March 1945 the Muslim Brotherhood opened their first Palestinian branch in Jerusalem. By 1947 it had more than 25 branches and 20,000 members in the mandate territory.[129] El-Husseini, who was not allowed to leave Egypt, was symbolically appointed President of the Muslim Brothers in Palestine and al-Banna's own deputy. His reputation as an Arab hero and leader of the Palestinians was thereby restored. "About one in every ten Arabs is a follower of the Mufti," wrote the *Magazine of the Year* in 1948, "and... it is unwise to criticise Hajj Amin in public."[130]

In May 1946 a Commission set up by the USA and Britain recommended the immediate emigration of 100,000 Holocaust survivors to Palestine. The Muslim Brothers' answer was wholly

127. El-Awaisi, op. cit., p. 195.
128. El-Awaisi, op. cit., p. 199.
129. El-Awaisi, op. cit., pp. 155ff and Mitchell, op. cit., p. 56.
130. Gensicke, op. cit., p. 143.

unambiguous, "Seventy million Arabs and 400 million Muslims behind them, with the Muslim Brothers in their forefront, would make the implementation of the Report impossible. Blood would flow like rivers in Palestine, ... so that it would not fall as an easy prey to Zionist vagabonds."[131] In the very same month the Muslim Brothers in Egypt organized a general strike against the Anglo-American Commission and, in the name of Egypt's King Farouk, called a conference of Arab kings, princes and heads of state. The Brotherhood could credit the meeting's rejection of the Commission's recommendations as a success.[132]

In the spring of 1947, the United Nations terminated the British mandate and established the United Nations Special Committee on Palestine (UNSCOP). After the failure of internal UN attempts to disqualify el-Husseini for his collaboration with the Nazis, the Committee invited both the Jewish Agency and the Mufti to make submissions. El-Husseini however boycotted the UN on the grounds that it was dominated by "imperialist interests." He also refused to meet envoys despatched to Cairo for unofficial discussions on the possibility of partition. Instead of this, "Hajj Amin, while he spoke more liberally to British emissaries, made it clear to other Arab leaders that, as soon as British forces were withdrawn, the Arabs should with one accord fall upon the Jews and destroy them."[133] The conflict now intensified. Even before the partition plan had been agreed upon, al-Banna ordered jihad and sent an initial battalion of volunteers to Palestine.

On November 29, 1947 the United Nations General Assembly, with the support of the USSR and Eastern bloc countries, decided on the long anticipated partition: 56% of the mandate territory was assigned to the Jewish state (for 500,000 Jews and

131. El-Awaisi, op. cit., p. 184.
132. El-Awaisi, op. cit., p. 185.
133. Nicholas Bethell, *The Palestinian Triangle. The struggle between the British, the Jews and the Arabs 1935-48* (London: Andre Deutsch Ltd., 1979), p. 349.

500,000 Arabs) and 43% to the Arab state (750,000 Arabs and 10,000 Jews); Jerusalem was to be placed under international jurisdiction.[134] As had previously happened with the 1937 Peel Commission recommendations, the Jews accepted this plan, while Husseini's party flatly rejected it. So what about the rest of the Arab World?

Outwardly, the Arab League vehemently fought against this two-state solution. However, as new archival findings have shown, it would be wrong to assume that all Arab leaders were united in rejecting the partition plan. For example, at that time, Abdullah, Emir of Jordan, privately declared that, "the partition of Palestine is the only realistic solution to the conflict."[135] Abd al-Rahman Azzam, the head of the Arab League, stated in 1947: "There is only one solution: the partition of Palestine." But of course he could not admit to this position publicly. Privately, the Egyptian Prime Minister of the day, Sidqi Pasha, also expressed a wish to accept the plan. According to his negotiating partner, Eliyahu Sasson, Pasha "repeatedly emphasized that he is a business man. His concern is the prosperity of Egypt. If a Jewish-Arab understanding contributes to this prosperity, then so be it."[136] And finally, here is Muzahim al-Pashashi, then Prime Minister of Iraq: "Eventually, he admitted, there would have to be an acceptance of the Jewish state's existence, but for now it was politically impossible to acknowledge this publicly. To do so, he said, would cause a revolt in Iraq."[137]

As early as November 30, the day after the vote, Arab guerrillas launched armed attacks on Jewish settlers and institutions. By the end of December, 205 Jews and 122 Arabs had been killed.[138]

134. Van der Meulen, op. cit., pp. 106ff.
135. See Thomas Mayer, Arab Unity of Action and the Palestine Question 1945-48, in: Middle Eastern Studies, Vol. 22, No. 3, July 1986, p. 344.
136. Cited in Michael Doran, *Pan-Arabism before Nasser,*(New York: Oxford University Press, 1999), p. 99
137. Cited in Bruse Maddy-Weitzman, The Crystallization of the Arab State System 1945-1954, New York: Syracuse University Press, 1993, p. 80.
138. Van der Meulen, op. cit., p. 108.

At the same time, Egypt witnessed the largest pro-Palestinian demonstration in its history. Over 100,000 people marched through the streets and applauded speakers who expressed their hope that Palestine could be liberated through bloodletting. Jewish and European institutions were attacked and partially destroyed. "The Muslim Brotherhood," writes Gudrun Krämer, "must bear at least the moral responsibility for the new riots."[139] The massive rejection of the UN partition plan and the effortless mobilization for the anti-Zionist armed struggle - in 48 hours the Brothers had recruited over 2,000 volunteers for Palestine - show how successful their years of agitation had been.[140]

But what was happening in Palestine itself? Here, many Arabs accepted the partition because they knew "that the fight against partition was futile because the Arabs had no arms and the Jews had the support of the U.S. and Britain." Or because they were among the "tens of thousands of labourers who advanced the Jewish economy, especially by working in the citrus groves."[141] "Many Palestinian Arabs thus not only refrained from fighting themselves, but also did their best to prevent foreigners and locals from carrying out military actions" writes Hillel Cohen, the first scholar to systematically investigate the movement of so-called Arab "collaborators." "Avoidance of war and even agreement with the Jews were, in their view, best for the Palestinian Arab nation."[142]

Just as in the 1936-39 civil war, a large part of the Mufti's effort was devoted to attacking fellow Palestinians who stood in his way. Among them was Fawzi Darwish Husseini, one of his cousins, who at the end of 1946 had wanted to sign an agreement on a binational state with representatives of the Jewish Agency based on the principle that no nation should dominate the other.

139. Krämer, op. cit., pp. 410ff and Mayer, op. cit., p. 107.
140. El-Awaisi, op. cit., p. 196 and Mitchell, p. 56.
141. Hillel Cohen, op. cit., p. 264.
142. Hillel Cohen, op. cit., p. 259.

On November 11, 1946 five members of the Fawzi group signed an agreement on common activities with the Jews. Twelve days later Fawzi was murdered by the Mufti's henchmen and his group disintegrated.[143] Then there was Sami Taha, a prominent Arab trade union leader in Haifa, who had expressed sympathy for an Arab-Jewish state; he was killed by the Mufti's men in September 1947.[144] Fawzi al-Qawuqji too remained a resolute opponent of the Mufti. He belonged to the commanders of the "Arab revolt" of the 1930s and was financed by the Arab League. In 1948 he found himself obliged to devote the bulk of his forces to keeping the Mufti's guerrillas in check. Unlike el-Husseini, Qawuqji was prepared to cooperate with the Zionists. In March 1948 he met a leading representative of the Jewish Agency and proposed a ceasefire and, after the withdrawal of the British, a Jewish-Arab federation under his leadership. In order to eliminate him from the game, the Mufti's Cairo office withheld money and weapons intended for Qawuqji' s troops and sent them to the Mufti's own followers instead.[145] The influential Nashashibi clan, who preferred to see Palestine divided rather than lose everything, continued to oppose the Mufti. The Nashashibis' most important ally was King Abdullah of Transjordan, who was also interested in a peaceful solution of the Jewish-Arab conflicts of interest and who had in the Second World War fought with the British against the Nazis and their Palestinian allies. "Abdullah soon made the matter clear," wrote Golda Meir, at that time head of the Jewish Agency's political department, in her memoirs. "He would not join in any Arab attack on us. He would always remain our friend, he said, and like us he wanted peace more than anything else. After all, we had a common foe, the Mufti of Jerusalem."[146] Fired up by the pro-Mufti Muslim Brothers, the

143. Laqueur, op. cit., p. 267.
144. Laqueur, op. cit., p. 267.
145. Van der Meulen, op. cit., p. 111 and Gensicke, op. cit., p. 256.
146. Janet Wallach, John Wallach, Araft. *In the Eyes of the Beholder* (New York: Carol Publishing Group, 1990) p. 257.

other Arab leaders shunned Abdullah and expressed their support for el-Husseini as the "legitimate" leader of Palestine.[147]

Nobody, of course, had caused more harm to the people of Palestine than that very same Mufti of Jerusalem. In alliance with al-Banna's Brotherhood he had done all he could to torpedo Arab-Jewish cooperation based on equal rights, destroyed every partition plan with his intransigence and adopted tactics which almost inevitably drove the Arab population of Palestine into the refugee camps.

In agreement with the decision of the UN General Assembly, on May 14, 1948 in Tel Aviv, David Ben-Gurion proclaimed the foundation of the Jewish state of Palestine, named Israel. A few hours later, the armies of Egypt, Jordan, Iraq, Syria and Lebanon crossed the borders of Palestine. The General Secretary of the Arab League, Abd al-Rahman Azzam, who had previously let it be known privately that he considered the division of Palestine the only rational solution, now stood shoulder to shoulder with the Mufti; "this war," he declared on the day of the Arab attack "will be a war of annihilation and lead to a terrible massacre, about which people will speak in the future as they do about the massacres of the Mongols or Crusaders."[148]

The newly founded country now had no choice. It faced, as historian Benny Morris puts it, either defence or downfall, and downfall meant, given the profound Arab hostility to Zionism, the "possible repetition, albeit on a smaller scale, of the Holocaust."[149] At the end of this war, in January 1949, the Israelis were mourning the deaths of over 4,000 soldiers and 2,000 civilians. The defeat of the Arab armies, which gave no figures for their losses, was almost total, extremely humiliating and marked by the flight of almost 80% of the Arab population originally living in the new

147. In 1951 King Abdullah was murdered by one of the Mufti's thugs.
148. Van der Meulen, op. cit., p. 116.
149. Reiner Bernstein, *Geschichte des Staates Israel II. Von der Gründung 1948 bis heute* (Schwalbach/Ts.: Wochenschau-Verlag, 1998), p. 18.

state of Israel. The Palestinian refugee problem, writes Benny Morris, "arose as a product of the war, not of planning, on either the Jewish or the Arab side.... It was partly the result of malicious actions by Jewish commanders and politicians, but to a lesser extent Arab commanders and politicians were responsible for its creation through their orders and failures."[150]

In Egypt, however, where only a few decades previously, antisemitism had stood no chance, the government declared martial law and in the night of May 14-15, 1948 arrested 2,000 Jews, a good quarter of whom were still behind bars in June.[151] Although in 1948 the government did not indulge in any full-scale or sustained persecution of the Jews, in the wartime months the Jewish population had to endure attacks on cinemas, businesses and shops in their neighbourhoods as well as innumerable assaults on individuals, instigated by members of the Muslim Brotherhood.

This organization was in fact at the peak of its power in 1948. With a million members and sympathisers it had long since developed into a state within a state, with its own factories, weapons, schools, hospitals and military units and was thus a threat to the Egyptian constitutional order.[152] In December 1948 the Brotherhood was banned. Al-Banna believed he could descry in these measures too "the hidden fingers of 'international Zionism', communism, and the partisans or atheism and depravity."[153] In fact, however, the Egyptian government was trying to forestall an attempted putsch following its military defeat. After a member of the organization had murdered the Egyptian Prime Minister,

---

150. Bernstein, op. cit., p. 27 and Benny Morris, "Vertreibung, Flucht und Schutzbedürfnis. Wie 1948 das Problem der palästinensischen Flüchtlinge entstand" in *FAZ*, December 29, 2001.
151. Krämer, op. cit., p. 415.
152. Since 1940 al-Banna had been forming special paramilitary units of the Brotherhood, which systematically recruited Egpyptian army officers, established arms depots and provided the majority of the volunteer forces in the 1948 war. See el-Awaisi, p. 110.
153. Mitchell, op. cit., p. 70.

Mahmud Fahmi al-Nugrashi, the Brotherhood was systematically and ruthlessly persecuted and al-Banna killed in the street
in February 1949 by government agents. Islamism, however, was
not wiped out by the terror; instead it radicalized further in the
prisons, as the following chapters will show. Indeed, the Brothers
who managed to escape spread their message all the more effectively in their countries of exile.

A few months after Hassan al-Banna's murder, James Heyworth-Dunne, at that time Professor of Arabic and Middle East
civilizations at Georgetown University in Washington D.C.,
described what Egypt might have looked like had al-Banna
achieved his goal and taken power in Cairo. Although the word
"Islamism" was not in use when Heyworth-Dunne wrote his
piece, he foresaw the social regression that fifty years later has
become a reality of daily life in Afghanistan, Gaza and Iran. His
warning, issued back in 1950, brings home the extent of the Muslim Brotherhood's success since its leader's murder.

"Should the *ikhwan* acquire power," Heyworth-Dunne
wrote, "the women of Egypt, who have gradually emancipated
themselves from their old habits of seclusion, would be forced to
give up their European fashions, and return to their Islamic customs which, in fact, prevailed only until twenty-five years ago.
The use of the veil would become compulsory. No woman would
be allowed to wear colours in public. Social life in the towns
would change radically, for the fashionable bars, restaurants
and cabarets would close down; alcoholic drinks would not only
be withdrawn from sale and their importation forbidden, but
anyone found drinking liquor would be scourged according to
Islamic law. Theatres and cinemas would be closed down as un-
Islamic, and the majority of newspapers and periodicals would
be withdrawn from circulation for the same reason.... It would
be virtually impossible to purchase any English or French novels
as such works are condemned in advance as a powerful weapon
used by the West in order to undermine Islamic morals; they are

considered a part of a subtle method employed by foreigners to destroy Islam."[154]

When Heyworth-Dunne wrote these words, which seem so prophetic to us today, the seeds have already been sown for Islamism's greatest success of the 20th century, the Iranian Revolution. Since the start of the 1930s the Mufti of Jerusalem had drawn the Shiite clergy of Iran into his anti-Jewish campaign.[155] In 1937, when he was already an influential figure, Khomeini had linked up with with representatives of the Muslim Brotherhood. He began to read Hassan el-Banna's writings and discussed with the Brotherhood's emissaries for days on end. Khomeini would later make a special point of listening regularly to the Farsi-language broadcasts put out by the Nazis from Zeesen.

"Germany's Persian service was, during the war, to enjoy the widest possible audience in Iran and Iraq. Khomeini listened to the programs every evening," wrote Amir Taheri in his biography of the Iranian leader.

"Khomeini had brought with him a radio receiver set made by the British company Pye which he had bought from an Indian Muslim pilgrimage. The radio proved to be a good buy.... Many mullahs would gather at his home, often on the terrace, in the evenings to listen to Radio Berlin and the BBC."[156]

While Khomeini was certainly not an acolyte of Hitler, it is not unreasonable to suppose that his anti-Jewish outlook, which contributed so much to his popularity from the beginning of the 1960s onwards, had been shaped during the 1930s.[157]

---

154. J. Heyworth-Dunne, op. cit., p. 70.

155. Henner Fürtig, 'Die Bedeutung der iranischen Revolution von 1979 als Ausgangspunkt für eine antijüdisch orientierte Islamisierung', in Wolfgang Benz, ed., *Jahrbuch für Antisemitismusforschung* Vol. 12 (Berlin: Metropol, 2003), p. 76.

156. Amir Taheri, *The Spirit of Allah. Khomeini & the Islamic Revolution* (Bethesda, MA: Adler & Adler, 1986), pp. 98ff.

157. Matthias Küntzel, 'Iran's Obsession with the Jews. Denying the Holocaust, Desiring Another One', *Weekly Standard*, February 19, 2007, pp. 18-22.

What insights has our review of the origins of modern jihadism yielded? Firstly, it should be emphasized that the rise of Nazism and Islamism took place in the same period. This was no accident, for both movements represented attempts to answer the crisis of capitalism. However different their answers may have been, they shared a crucial central feature: in both cases the sense of belonging to a homogeneous community had been created through mobilizing for war and pogrom against the Jews.

Neither the Mufti nor the founders of the Muslim Brothers were creations of European fascism. However, both were strengthened by it. Like an elder brother, National Socialism had backed the fledgling Islamist movement up with catchwords, intellectual encouragement and money. With the "Cairo Jewish trial" the Nazis had exported their antisemitism to Egypt. Egyptian movements such as Young Egypt modelled their street processions on the Nazi mass marches. The Muslim Brotherhood got financial support from the German News Agency in Egypt. Again, it was thanks to supplies of money from the Nazis that the Mufti was able to sustain the uprising in Palestine, which al-Banna then used to boost the formation of his jihadi movement.

Secondly, we have learned that the escalation of the Palestine conflict did not have "natural" or "historically determined" roots, but was and is the result of a purposeful campaign. While Jewish fundamentalism has throughout been a minority force within Zionism, in the Arab camp the radical anti-Jewish current led by el-Husseini and al-Banna prevailed in bloody battles with its opponents. Their "holy war" never aimed to achieve a better life or individual happiness, but served a "higher" mission: the enforcement of an exclusive religious identity which eliminated everything foreign and ostracized even the hesitant as deserters.

Why of all issues did al-Banna choose Palestine as the most important instrument for re-establishing the principle of jihad as a duty for Muslims? As a religious duty, jihad required a religious justification. In the case of Palestine this prerequisite was present. The al-Aqsa mosque in Jerusalem was, after Mecca and Medina, orthodox Islam's third most holy pilgrimage site. Moreover, according to the *sunna*, it was precisely from Jerusalem that Muhammad had embarked on a mystical night journey into the heavens. Only the struggle over Palestine could be inflated into a life and death issue and serve as "the market where" - according to the Brotherhood's newspaper *al-Nadhir* - "we make a bargain by winning one of the two advantages, victory or martyrdom." Only Palestine offered the starting point from which the *umma*, the community of all the world's Muslims, could be united behind one and the same goal. And had not, according to tradition, Muhammad predicted a decisive battle for the *umma* "in Jerusalem and around it?"[158]

Thirdly, it should be pointed out that, alone, neither the Brotherhood nor the Mufti could have had the same influence on the course of the Palestine conflict as they would have together. After 1945 the Muslim Brothers helped el-Husseini to regain a leadership role, while under the rule of the Nashashibis in Palestine al-Banna's jihad would have been a derisory affair. In his study of 1950, J. Heyworth-Dunne summarized the significance of this alliance in the following way: "The real change for Hassan [al-Banna] came with the troubles in Palestine from 1936 on. He had contacted the Mufti, had become one of his keenest supporters, and had, no doubt, some kind of agreement with him, for it was his work in Palestine for the Arabs and the Mufti which changed the whole outlook of Hassan al-Banna's movement and policy. The Mufti thought very highly of Hassan, while the Mufti was the one person respected by the *ikhwan* leader."[159] In this historic alliance, al-Banna operated as a warlike priest using the Palestine conflict to unite the Islamic world for a new Caliphate, while the Mufti acted as a sophisticated tactician using Islam to further the "liberation" of Palestine (and thereby

158. El-Awaisi, op. cit., pp. 14ff.
159. J. Heyworth-Dunne, op. cit., p. 22.

his own power). However, it was in fact the religious figure who represented the urban element, pursuing mass politics with the most modern means of propaganda, while the Mufti stood for the rural population, clan roots, *sharia* terror and the formation of gangs. It was this interplay between the Egyptian-urban and Palestinian-rural elements that helped the Banna-Husseini tandem to extend its influence throughout the Arab world.

Fourthly, it is remarkable that since then the cohesion of the Arab world has been defined not by religion or a particular relationship to Britain or the USA, but by opposition to Zionism or more precisely Israel. Hatred of the Jews has become the most important shared bond. It was British policy on Palestine, not on oil, which determined whether friendship or enmity would prevail in Arab-British relations, just as today the USA is mainly criticized for its support to Israel. The bogeyman of the Israeli enemy also serves an internal political function: whenever anything goes amiss, it is blamed not on the domestic authorities, but on the apparently all-powerful enemy.

Fifthly, however, the history of the Muslim Brothers shows that revolutionary antisemitism is no mere supplementary feature of modern jihadism; it is its core. In the Brotherhood's early activities, antisemitism was mainly apparent as a structure of thought and worldview. Specific powers or groups were identified relatively interchangeably as responsible for the renunciation of former believers and the humiliation of Muslims and thus declared enemies: Communists, the West, Christian missionaries, hedonists, Zionists or the Suez Canal Company. The most important characteristic of this mode of thought was the rage at everything different, which invariably vented itself in action against the "other." Instead of accepting and valuing distinctions – and the acknowledgement of equality between women and men has always been the starting point of that acceptance – the Islamists' utopia was (and is) aimed at suppressing differences so as to extinguish individuality and submit everybody to the binding forces of the clan and the religion.

With the Brotherhood's Palestine campaign of 1936 a second stage began: now the Jews were identified as the main enemy. Passages from the Koran on the alleged inferiority of the Jews were mingled with frightful rumours from the British mandate territory and elements of European antisemitism, and forms of struggle such as the "boycott of Jews" adapted from Germany.

In 1945, we enter a third phase, as a world-conspiracy theory emerged out of pogromist antisemitism. Hassan al-Banna's anti-Americanism was a product of the USA's support for Zionism, for which he could find only one reason; "Jewish gold," "Zionist influence" and the "Zionist-dominated" opinion and education industries. The United Nations' involvement with Palestine too was for al-Banna no more than "a new declaration of the Zionist crusader war against the Arab and Islamic peoples." In this world-conspiracy theory, which, immediately after the closure of gas chambers, attempted to brand the Jews as the rulers of the world, the ideological convergence of the Muslim Brothers with National Socialism reached its culmination. As a result, the delusion suppressed in Germany after May 8, 1945 found its most fruitful exile in the Arab world, where the Muslim Brothers now disposed of a million followers.

CHAPTER TWO
· · · · · · · · · · · · · · ·
EGYPTIAN ISLAMISM FROM NASSER TO THE
PRESENT DAY

Has Amin el-Husseini, the Mufti of Jerusalem who died in 1974, risen from the dead? Comments in leading Egyptian newspapers suggested this might be so. "With regard to this Holocaust swindle, many French studies have shown that this is nothing more than a fabrication, a lie and a fraud," declared, for example, the Cairo columnist Fatma Abdullah Mahmoud on April 29, 2002. He continued, "But, I, personally, complain to Hitler, even saying to him from the bottom of my heart, 'If only you had done it, brother, if only it had really happened, so that the world could sigh in relief without their evil and sin.'"[160] This heartfelt wish to see all the Jews at last annihilated was published in the country's second largest daily, the Government-controlled *Al-Akhbar*.

Not only the Mufti, but Hassan al-Banna as well seems to have returned to present-day Egypt, together with his 1948 movement of volunteers for *jihad*. Thus, in March 2002, the Muslim Brothers announced that they had set up secret training camps for volunteer suicide bombers. Enrolment in the program was going strong. Only two days after the start of the registration process, 2,000 students had already placed their names on the list of those ready to die blowing up Israelis. A month later the new movement could celebrate its first "martyr for the Palestinian cause", shot by Israeli soldiers, and rename schools in

160. Cited in *Middle East Media Research Institute* (MEMRI) *Report* no 375, May 3, 2002. Previously, in April 2001 *Al-Akhbar* had repeatedly printed the complaint that Hitler had not sufficiently "avenged" himself on the Jews. See *MEMRI Reports* nos. 208 and 212.

his memory. "In Egypt the Islamists have assumed the ideological leadership", was the *Frankfurter Allgemeine Zeitung*'s accurate summary of the situation.[161]

It is by no means obvious why this return to the 1930s and 1940s should have occurred. Contemporary circumstances differ significantly from those of the former period. Modern jihadism first arose in the context and with the support of Nazism, which had suffered military defeat in 1945. So how did Islamism come through this defeat unscathed and go on to become ideologically dominant in present-day Egypt? Had not the celebrated Gamal Abdel Nasser successfully crushed the Islamists and from the mid-1950s turned Egypt into the anti-imperialist model for the Non-Aligned Movement? Had not his successor Anwar as-Sadat been awarded the Nobel Peace Prize for making peace with Israel? And has not the current leader, Hosni Mubarak, in power since 1981, been praised for his steps to curb Islamism? Egypt is the most influential power in the Arab world and the country from which modern jihadism stemmed. Moreover, Egypt has continued to exert a decisive influence on Islamism's further development up to and including the foundation of al-Qa'ida.

The following sections look at the metamorphoses of Egyptian Islamism since 1948. The decisive event that determined everything that came after took place in 1967. "The historical shift in favour of Islamism began with the third Arab-Israeli war, the Six-Day War of 1967", notes Bassam Tibi, expressing the consensus among students of Islamism.[162] Indeed! The defeat of the Arab armies by Israel turned out to be *the* historical watershed in the embedding of the jihadi idea. What is the explanation for

161. MEMRI Special Dispatch no. 363, April 7, 2002; Max Rodenbeck, "Taking the Tragedy Personally", *International Herald Tribune* (IHT), April 18, 2002; Tim Golden, "Young Egyptians Hearing Call of 'Martyrdom'2 *NYT*, April 26, 2002; Rainer Hermann, "Suche nach dem Konsens", *FAZ*, July 8, 2002.
162. Bassam Tibi, *Kreuzzug und Djihad. Der Islam und die Christliche Welt* (Munich: Goldmann, 2001b), pp. 243ff.

the coincidence of military debacle and the rise in support for Islamism? Why was it Islamism rather than any other ideology which profited from defeat by the Jewish state? So let us begin with Gamal Abdul Nasser and his defeat in the Six-Day War.

The Humiliation

In 1952 Gamal Abdel Nasser headed the July Revolution of the "Free Officers," which abolished the monarchy, proclaimed a republic, dissolved the existing parties and deprived the old elites of power. Together with Pandit Nehru (India), Ahmed Sukarno (Indonesia) and Josip Tito (Yugoslavia), Nasser belonged to the founders of the bloc of non-aligned states whose aim was to pursue an independent development path by exploiting the contradictions between NATO and the Warsaw Pact. Nasser became an Arab anti-colonialist hero when in 1956 he nationalized the Suez Canal in the face of British and French resistance. Shortly thereafter Israel attacked Egypt in the so-called Sinai war. At virtually the same time French and British troops intervened with the goal of re-establishing control over the Suez Canal.[163] Although in fact it was the attitude of the USA and Soviet Union, rather than the Egyptian army, which compelled the European powers and Israel to withdraw, it was President Nasser who emerged from the crisis as the sole political victor.

163. A "major deciding factor" in the launch of the Israeli campaign of 1956 was the strengthening of Egyptian military positions in Sinai "together with a sharp increase in the number of murder and sabotage attacks on Israeli territory" reports S. Barel in "Tatsachen zum Nahostkonflikt", in Michael Landmann, *Das Israel-Pseudos der Pseudolinken* (Berlin: Colloquium Verlag, 1971) op. cit., p. 134. While Moshe Dayan, head of the Israeli General Staff, wanted to strike back in 1955, President Ben-Gurion linked military action to support from several great powers. This support was provided in 1956 by France and Britain, who wanted to force Nasser to rescind the nationalization of the Suez Canal by military force. See Naor, op. cit., p. 333. No other action in Israeli history, of course, lent more apparent support to the conspiracy theory promulgated by the Soviet Union and Egypt that Israel was an agent of imperialism in the Arab region.

In 1967 Nasser felt himself politically and militarily strong enough to follow up his closure of the Suez Canal to Israeli shipping with that of the Gulf of Aqaba and to amass troops in Sinai. On May 20, 1967 Nasser explained the reasons for his actions on Cairo Radio: "With the closure of the Gulf of Aqaba, Israel has but two alternatives, either of which will destroy it. It will either be throttled by the Arab economic blockade or destroyed under the fire of Arab military forces." "Our basic objective", he reiterated later to a meeting of Arab trade unionists, "will be to destroy Israel."[164]

Israel's response to the acute threat to its existence has gone down in history as the Six-Day War. The Israeli army succeeded on the very first day in eliminating the Egyptian airforce as it readied for take-off, thereby dealing the united forces of Egypt, Syria and Jordan a crushing blow. The psychological impact of this defeat is to be explained not only by the fact that it ignominiously and unexpectedly shattered Nasser's aura of invincibility. Far more critical was the fact that it had been none other than the Jews, derided by Muslims as "enfeebled and cowardly", who had defeated the Arab armies. A glance at the early history of Islam in the seventh century will help us understand why pious Muslims experienced the six-day war as a well-nigh unbearable humiliation.

In the Christian mythology which inspired the medieval anti-Jewish pogroms in Europe the Jews were constantly depicted as a dark and demonic force. This ascription had a simple origin: since the Jews had been able to murder even the Son of God, nothing else in the field of cosmic malice was beyond them. All the fairy-tales about the deadly and powerful Jewish force derive from this Christian original. Muslim anti-Jewish prejudice on the other hand stems from a wholly different story, that of Muham-

---

164. Michael Landmann, op. cit., p. 72 and Walter Laqueur, Barry Rubin (eds.) *The Israel-Arab Reader. A Documentary History of the Middle East Conflict* (New York: Penguin Books, 1984), p. 176.

mad's experiences with the Jews of Medina. In this case it was not the Jews who defeated the Son of God, but the Prophet who emerged the clear victor.

In 622 Muhammad, finding no support for his ideas in Mecca, was compelled to make the so-called *hijra*, the migration to Medina. In that city, known at the time as Yathrib, there lived some 10,000 Jews, divided into three tribes, the Qurayza, the Nadir and the Qaynuqa. The strong Jewish presence contributed to the fact that Muhammad's monotheistic message found an audience there.[165] Relations between the Jews and Muhammad's followers changed in 624, when Muhammad, following a victory over the Meccans, wished to convert the Qaynuqa by force. The latter refused and were then expelled from the city. The Nadir tribe met the same fate in 625. This time Muhammad had suffered a defeat at the hands of the Meccans and wanted to restore his shaken authority at the Nadir's expense. In 627 the Qurayza tribe was exterminated following a siege of Medina by the Meccans. "Muhammad went to the marketplace in Medina and had graves dug there. Then the Jews were brought to him and beheaded at the gravesides – between 600 and 900 men in all. The executions lasted the whole day…. Most of the women and children were sold into slavery in Medina, the remainder in Syria and Nadjad.[166] Subsequently, Islamic tradition justified Muhammad's measures against the Jews of Medina by reference to certain misdeeds the latter were alleged to have committed. In the first case, some of the Qaynuqa were accused of having killed a Muslim. In the case of the Nadir, a Jewish family was said to have been preparing an attack on Muhammad. Finally, it was claimed that the Qurayza had entered into an alliance with the Meccans.[167]

165. Johan Bouman, *Der Koran und die Juden*, (Darmstadt: Wissenschaftliche Buchgesellschaft, 1990), S. 56 und 59.
166. Johan Bouman, op. cit., p. 86.
167. Carl Brockelmann, *Geschichte der islamischen Völker und Staaten*, (München und Berlin: R. Oldenbourg, 1939), pp. 19-24.

These events and their interpretation shaped the Muslim view of Jews in three ways. Firstly, Islam considers the Jews to be even more hostile than the Christians. In the words of the Koran: "The Jews and polytheists are the worst enemies of the believers" (sura 5, verse 85).[168] While, however, the classical Islamic literature treats the struggle with the Jews as a relatively minor episode in the life of the Prophet, for the last 70 years, Muhammad's conflict with the Jews has been portrayed as a central theme in his career, and their alleged enmity to him "given a cosmic significance."[169] Secondly, Muslim preachers have cited the expulsion and killing of the Jews of Medina as the model for policy towards Israel. And, thirdly, the ease with which Muhammad allegedly overcame the Jews and inflicted condign punishment on them marked them as being a weak enemy, an object more of ridicule than of fear.

Both these factors - on the one hand the Muslim domination fantasy based on the conviction of possessing the only true divine revelation and, on the other, the specific stereotype of the Jews as cowardly and weak - need to be borne in mind, if one is to appreciate the shock created by the Israeli victory in 1967 throughout the Arab world. The collective sense of profound humiliation was huge and cried out both for someone to blame and for interpretation. Both were provided by religion.

Already in the summer of 1967 Muslim religious leaders from 33 countries met in Cairo for "The fourth conference of the al-Azhar Academy of Islamic Research" to discuss the causes of the defeat and what was in their eyes the especially painful

---

168. As "people of the Book (the Bible)", Jews and Christians have since the eighth century been considered in the Islamic world as dhimmi (= protected people), with a special, but inferior status. In general, the Muslim attitude to them was "that of a ruling people which was prepared to show a certain generosity towards a subject people, as long as they behaved with appropriate humility." Jews, for example, were not allowed to bear weapons or ride horses and had to wear special distinctive clothing. The use of yellow markings for Jews did not originate in mediaeval Europe, but in Baghdad. See Bernard Lewis, op. cit., pp. 126ff and Robert Wistrich, *Muslim Antisemitism; a Clear and Present Danger* (American Jewish Committee, Washington 2002), p. 4.

169. Bernard Lewis, op. cit., p. 128.

"loss of Jerusalem." The conclusions of this authoritative body were crystal clear: in the view of this assembly the defeat in the June war was proof that Nasser's "Islamic socialism" was not in accordance with Allah's wishes and that, therefore, redemption from the disgrace could only be achieved through a renewed and intensified return to the faith. The anti-Jewish components of Islam were now invested with new life and vigour - not only by the leaders of the Muslim Brotherhood but by the religious leaders of the Islamic world.[170]

Guidance from the religious elite, however, is not a sufficient answer to the question of why Islamism became hegemonic after 1967. A second element of an answer can be found in Nasser's biography. For it was Nasser, who remained in office until his death in September 1970, who himself set in motion the turn to Islam. Below we look at certain key aspects of Nasser's life which have been carefully airbrushed out of the record by hagiographers of the Soviet school, for instance his membership of the Muslim Brotherhood.

Comrade Brother Nasser

In the 1930s Nasser, born in 1918, was politically moulded by the Young Egypt movement, which was sympathetic to National Socialism and of which he was a member.[171] At the beginning of the 1940s his career was sponsored by Hitler's most prominent supporter in Egypt, General Aziz al-Misri.[172] Nasser was later able to repay the debt: in 1942 at British instigation Aziz-al-Misri and Egyptian prime minister Ali Mahir were dismissed because

170. D.F. Green, ed., *Arab Theologians on Jews and Israel* (Genève: Editions de l'Avenir, 1971); Yvonne Haddad, "Islamists and the 'Problem of Israel': the 1967 Awakening," in *Middle East Journal*, volume 46, no, 2, pp. 278ff. James Jankowski, "Nasserism and Egyptian State Policy 1952-1958," in James Jankowski, Israel Gershoni, *Rethinking Nationalism in the Arab Middle East* (New York: Columbia University Press, 1997), p. 151.
171. James Jankowski, op. cit., p. 151.
172. Kirk J. Beattie, *Egypt during the Nasser Years. Ideology, Politics and Civil Society* (New York: Westview Press, 1994), p. 45.

of their explicitly pro-German stance. Ten years later both were reinstated by the Free Officers coup: while al-Misri was hailed as the "spiritual father" of the July Revolution, the officers made Ali Mahir the new prime minister.[173]

The leader of the Muslim Brotherhood, Hassan al-Banna, was friendly with Aziz al-Misri and in 1940 arranged meetings between him and Nasser's friend and successor, Anwar as-Sadat. In 1941 Sadat joined the Brotherhood's military organization and in 1943/44 Nasser and other officers followed suit. Between 1944 and 1948 these officers had weekly meetings with the Muslim Brothers' military chief, Mahmud Labib, and took part in the clandestine military training of volunteers for the 1947-48 war in Palestine. Nasser's circle of friends also included Amin el-Husseini, the former Mufti of Jerusalem, whom he asked to persuade King Farouk to allow Egyptian officers to take part in the fighting in Palestine. In 1948 Gamal Abdel Nasser was a commander on the Palestinian front.

The preparations for the 1952 military coup took place in very close coordination with the Muslim Brothers, which had been legalized in 1951. Nasser offered to confer total power on the Brotherhood, but this plan was dropped out of fear of British military intervention.

On the very eve of the coup Nasser reaffirmed his oath of fealty to the Muslim Brothers and promised, at least gradually, to introduce *sharia* law.[174]

When on 22 July the Free Officers revolution triumphed, it was correctly interpreted as a victory for the Muslim Brothers. Ten of the 14 putschists who now ruled Egypt had declared their loyalty to the Brotherhood. The Soviet Union at first condemned the coup as "fascist" and the junta as a "reactionary regime controlled by Washington." Nasser offered the most prominent

173. Beattie, op. cit., pp. 45 and 69.
174. Beattie, op. cit., pp. 47ff and 57. See also Mitchell, op. cit., p. 96; Jbara, op. cit., p. 190.

Brother of the time, Sayyid Qutb, a variety of senior government posts, albeit in vain.[175] In January 1953, with the acclaim of the Brotherhood, all parties and organizations apart from them were banned.

Soon however relations between the Brotherhood and the Revolutionary Council began to sour. The Brothers realized that Nasser attached far more importance to the improvement of secular education and land reform than to the introduction of *sharia* law. Moreover, in March 1954 Egypt signed its first trade agreement with the Soviet Union, a country for which the Brothers felt particular contempt. Further agreements were to follow. In October 1954 the attempted assassination of Nasser by a Muslim Brother marked the definitive end of friendly relations. Now the Brotherhood too was banned, thousands of its members jailed and its Cairo headquarters set ablaze. The end of 1954 saw the beginning of the phase in the Muslim Brothers' history known by them as *al-mihna* (catastrophe), played out in the regime's prisons and torture chambers, an experience not without effect on Islamism theory and practice.[176]

Despite the repression, Nasser remained loyal to some of the Brotherhood's ideological principles. Prior to the consolidation of Soviet influence in Egypt, the country's new rulers had made no secret of their Nazi sympathies. It was not by chance that Egypt became the El Dorado of former Nazis who decamped there in droves in the 1950s. The Free Officers welcomed them with open arms, not for humanitarian reasons, but out of political conviction. Thus Anwar as-Sadat in 1953, when rumours were circulating that Hitler was still alive, wrote a tribute to

175. J. Beattie, op. cit., pp. 72ff. A. Bennigsen, Paul B. Henze, George K. Tanham, S. E. Winbush, *Soviet Strategy and Islam* (London: Palgrave Macmillan, 1989), p. 83 and Gudrun Krämer, *Gottes Staat als Republik. Reflexionen zeitgenössischer Muslime zu Islam. Menschenrechten und Demokratie* (Baden-Baden: Nomos-Verlagsgesellschaft, 1999), pp. 212ff.
176. Dilip Hiro, *Holy Wars. The Rise of Islamic Fundamentalism* (New York, Routledge, 1989), p. 66. Bennigsen et al., op. cit., pp. 83ff and Mitchell, op. cit., p. 152; Krämer 1999, op. cit., p. 195.

the Führer. "My dear Hitler," he declared, "I congratulate you from the bottom of my heart. Even if you appear to have been defeated, in reality you are the victor. ...You may be proud of becoming the immortal leader of Germany. We will not be surprised if you appear again in Germany or if a new Hitler rises up in your wake."[177]

Out of consideration for his Soviet friends, Nasser refrained from expressions of sympathy for Hitler. Things were different when it came to his obsession with Israel and the Jews. In his study of Arab antisemitism, Bernard Lewis reveals the enormously wide circulation and popularity in the Arab world of the antisemitic defamation, the *Protocols of the Elders of Zion*, emphasising that, "In President Nasser's day, the main source of such propaganda was Egypt."[178]

In 1957 Nasser had for the first time publicly recommended the reading of the Protocols. According to the Egyptian President, this text "proves beyond a shadow of doubt that three hundred Zionists, each of whom knows all the others, govern the fate of the European continent." Subsequently, the Protocols were extolled by senior government figures in semi-governmental publications, and quasi-official pamphlets were published

177. Wistrich 1987, op. cit., p. 314.
178. Bernard Lewis, op. cit., p. 210. There currently exist 60 Arabic versions of the Protocols which can be bought in every urban bookshop in the Arab world. See Wistrich 2002, op. cit., p. 21. The Protocols were compiled between 1894 and 1899 in France and disseminated in Russia from 1903 onwards by far right circles and are claimed to be the translation of the minutes of a meeting of a "World Union of the Freemasons and the Elders of Zion." The text sets out – in the form of speeches of the leader of a "Jewish secret government" - the methods and goals of the "Jewish conspiracy": manipulation of the masses, incitement of party conflicts and labour unrest, spreading of Liberal ideas, corruption of morals and the unleashing of terror and war. Radiating out from Germany, the influence of the Protocols spread like wildfire across the world after 1920. Since 1935 the fact that this is a forgery has been legally attested. See Michael Hagemeister, "'Die Protokolle der Weisen von Zion' and der Basler Zionistenkongress von 1897," in Heiko Haumann (ed.), *Der Erste Zionistenkongress von 1897 - Ursachen, Bedeutung, Aktualität* (Basle, 1997), pp. 336ff.

offering "proof" the United States was in reality a dependent of Israel.[179]

Just like the Muslim Brothers, Nasser denied the reality of the Holocaust. In an interview published in the *Deutsche Nationalzeitung* on May 1, 1964 he emphasized that, "During the Second World War, our sympathies were with the Germans.... The lie of the six million murdered Jews is not taken seriously by anybody."[180] Evidently, Nasser's anti-imperialism and his relations with the Soviet Union on one hand and his antisemitism and Holocaust-denial on the other hand proved remarkably compatible up until 1967.[181]

It was not until 1967 that Nasser's former career as a Muslim Brother began once more to influence his policies. The conclusions that Nasser drew from the defeat of his armed forces were in line with his obsessional hatred of Jews and taste for conspiracy theories.

First conclusion: the Arabs were not defeated by the Israeli armed forces, but had in reality been the victim of the great powers. "It became very clear from the first moment that there were other powers behind the enemy. ... We were the victims of a diplomatic trick, a political deception in which we had not imagined a major Power would involve itself," he declared as early as June 9, 1967.

Second conclusion: on to the next war! In the summer of 1967 the Israeli government offered to withdraw from the territories it had occupied in exchange for a peace treaty. On September 1, 1967 this offer was answered by the Arab summit in Khartoum by a threefold "no": No to peace with Israel, no to the recognition of Israel, no to talks with Israel. Instead, preparations for a new war were intensified. On July 23, 1968 Nasser stated, "Life will be

179. Wistrich 1987, op. cit., p. 317. Lewis, op. cit., p. 253.
180. Lewis, op. cit., p. 194.
181. For an account of the "springtide of antisemitism" in the socialist bloc countries following destalinization in the Soviet Union in 1956, see Wistrich 1987, op. cit., pp. 355ff. The mutual relationship between Soviet anti-Zionism and Arab antisemitism, remains, to my knowledge, unexplored.

meaningless and worthless to us until every inch of Arab soil is liberated.... The battle against the enemy must have priority over everything else."

Third conclusion: God had punished the Arabs with this defeat because they had strayed from the path of righteousness. On July 23, 1967, Nasser stated: "Perhaps Almighty God wanted to give us a lesson ... to cleanse our souls from the blemishes that have affected us and the shortcomings that we must avoid as we build our new society."[182] It was Nasser himself, who after the June war, unexpectedly fell back on Islamic rhetoric and initiated the religious turn which continues to this day.

Under Nasser, Egyptian officers were furnished educational material on the meaning of jihad and Muhammad's campaigns. Under Nasser, the state-controlled media were ordered to give Islam extensive airtime and a radio station exclusively dedicated to the recitation of the Koran was launched. In April 1968 several hundred Muslim Brothers were given amnesty and for the first time Muslim and Christian children separated in schools.[183] Nasser always reacted to changes in his political environment as a chameleon. Its dominant range of colours however - fascism, anti-imperialism and Islamism - were already present in the program of the Muslim Brothers.

"The historic shift towards jihadi Islamism" of which Bassam Tibi speaks is, therefore, attributable to two factors. Firstly, to the humiliation resulting from the Arab armies' defeat and secondly, by Nasser's interpretation of this crisis, which drew on his Islamist roots and ran along the tracks laid down by el-Husseini and al-Banna. In 1970 Nasser died a natural death. His successor Anwar as-Sadat, however, was murdered by Islamists in 1981. In the course of these eleven years, the country underwent a further change.

182. Nasser's speeches can be found in Laqueur/Rubin, op. cit., pp. 190ff.
183. Dilip Hiro, op. cit., p. 69; see also Neil MacFarquhaur, "Egyptian Group Patiently Pursues Dream of Islamic State," *NYT*, January 30, 2002.

Islamism under Sadat

When Nasser died, 15,000 Soviet advisers and military experts were stationed in Egypt.[184] Sadat swiftly packed them off back to their homeland and opened up Egyptian markets to international capital. The private sector was fostered and the land reform gradually rescinded. Social tensions intensified. In 1974 the inflation rate reached 24%. Chronic supply problems, a rising cost of living, housing shortage, high unemployment, lack of opportunities for university graduates, and in contrast, a new bourgeoisie which insensitively flaunted its wealth, provoked unrest and mass protests such as the spontaneous "bread revolt" at the beginning of 1977.[185]

In order to divert these protests against his economic policies toward religious channels, Sadat forged ahead with the turn to Islam initiated by Nasser.

His government set up hundreds of Islamic associations in the factories to combat atheistic Marxism. In the universities religious groups were promoted in order to establish, as he believed, a more easily controllable counterweight to socialist and Communist groups. Nationalism and Pan-Arabism were replaced at all levels by a return to Islam and the universalistic umma-concept.[186]

Sadat decreed that the state-controlled radio and TV stations, media that could reach the illiterate masses, should broadcast prayers five times a day and devote ample airtime to diverse religious programmes.[187] Mosques sprang from the ground as if they were coming off a conveyor belt: during his eleven-year rule the number of mosques more than doubled from 20,000 (1970) to 46,000 (1981), of which only 6,000 were under state control.[188] On September 11, 1971, thirty years to the day before the assault

184. Beattie, op. cit., p. 225.
185. Kogelmann, op. cit., p. 84.
186. Hiro, op. cit., p. 70.
187. Hiro, op. cit., p. 70.
188. Kogelmann, op. cit., p. 168.

on the World Trade Centre and Pentagon, it was transcribed into the Egyptian constitution that in the future "the principles of *sharia*" would be regarded as "a major source of legislation." In 1980 the indefinite was replaced by the definite article so that ever since the *sharia* has been considered not just "a," but "the" main source of legislation.[189]

The Islamism of the Muslim Brothers in particular was deliberately given a new lease of life. In the summer of 1971 Sadat offered the Brotherhood's exile groups full guarantees of freedom in Egypt. Between 1973 and 1975 all the Muslim Brothers held in Egypt's jails were released, a measure that created a sensation in the Arab world.[190] Until his visit to Jerusalem in 1977, relations between Sadat and the Islamists, who could operate and grow comparatively freely, were marked by "total harmony."[191]

Under Sadat students developed into the most important support-base of a new Islamist movement: since the mid-1970s, all student representative bodies in Egyptian universities have been dominated by radical Islamist groups.[192] The *gama'at al-islamiyya* (Islamic Societies), founded by the former Muslim Brother Sukri Mustafa in 1973, has established itself as the most significant organization.

Mustafa's development is typical of the radicalized element of his generation. Born in 1942 he was jailed for the first time as an activist in the Muslim Brotherhood at the age of 23 and granted amnesty in 1971 under Sadat. In the meantime, in the Nasser regime's prison camps, the incarcerated Brothers had engaged in a wide-ranging theoretical discussion. Through these debates,

189. Tibi 2001a, op. cit., p. 304.
190. Serauky, op. cit., p. 47.
191. According to Gilles Kepel, *Das Schwarzbuch des Dschihad. Aufstieg und Niedergang des Islamismus* (Munich: Piper, 2002), p. 105. See also Kogelmann, op. cit., pp. 82 and 89.
192. Ulrike Dufner, *Islam ist nicht Islam. Die türkische Wohlfahrtspartei und die ägyptische Muslimbruderschaft: Ein Vergleich ihrer politischen Vorstellungen vor dem gesellschaftspolitischen Hintergrund* (Opladen: Leske + Budrich, 1998), p. 67.

under the influence of the ideas of Qutb (examined below), new radical Islamist groups formed who considered the Muslim Brotherhood's policies too reformist. This current, of which the *gama'at* was only one expression, viewed the entire Egyptian society as being in a state of unprecedented faithlessness. This conclusion stemmed not the least from their concrete situation: could the torturers at whose mercy they found themselves really be Muslims? Could a ruler such as Nasser, who ordered the torture, be a Muslim? Had not all those who obeyed these unbelieving leaders, in reality long ago renounced the faith?

As a result of these deliberations some of the groups hermetically sealed themselves off from the outside world in order to establish Islamist counter-societies of true believers. Others promoted Islamism in the universities, skilfully combining the provision of basic services with religious propaganda. Thus, drawing on subsidies of undetermined origin, the Islamists were able to offer female students "Islamic apparel" (veils, long white coats and gloves) at knock-down prices. As long as they wore the veil, women students had access to women-only transport free of charge. At the same time, sexual segregation was increasingly introduced in the lecture halls.[193]

Some in Europe tend to romanticize such practices as a fascinating expression of defiance against the West. Their implications, however, are more disturbing. It is not easy for secularized people steeped in the principles of the Enlightment to comprehend the strange premises of orthodox Islam. However, the effort has to be made.

Unity and Submission

First of all, let us clarify our terms: *orthodox* Islam and *reformist* Islam differ from one another through the answer they give to the question of whether the old religion must be re-interpreted

---

193. Kepel, op. cit., p. 104.

or only revived. While secularized Muslims look at the sacred text in the context of its historical origins and thus oppose its full application to present-day conditions, Islamists take the Koran literally and adapt it with the aim of solving all contemporary problems.[194]

Between *Islamism* and *orthodox Islam* there are more similarities than differences. They are in broad agreement, for example, on the content of belief and the forms of religious ritual. Islamists, however, do not attach much importance to the latter, since in their eyes something else is more important: the struggle against the unbelievers. Jihadis wage this struggle arms in hand, exploiting every advance in military technology. While jihadism and radical Islamism are synonymous, the difference between Islamists and orthodox believers lies mainly in the conclusions drawn from their beliefs: the boundaries being fluid.[195] So what defines the common worldview of Islamists and orthodox Muslims?

The first and most important premise concerns Islamic epistemology. Even the apparently banal claim that human reason is the basic source of knowledge and scientific progress is considered sacrilegious by orthodox Muslims. According to their doctrine, human beings are incapable of producing knowledge. In their strive for knowledge they are merely granted the privilege of more accurately discerning God's will – the only real source of knowledge – through study of the holy texts in order to bring their own behavior into accordance with it. Religious faith and knowledge are thus one and the same, since deeper knowledge is nothing other than a constantly clearer interpretation of the signs given by God.[196]

194. Johannes J. G. Jansen, *The Dual Nature of Islamic Fundamentalism* (London: Hurst & Company, 1997), p. 29.
195. Jansen, op. cit., pp. 9ff. Bassam Tibi defines Islamism as "an ideology of open or (consciously) concealed jihadist confrontation." Tibi 2001a, p. 247.
196. Bassam Tibi, *Islamischer Fundamentalismus, moderne Wissenschaft und Technologie* (Frankfurt am Main: Suhrkamp, 1992), p. 87.

No Islamist is therefore doubtful that the statement in the Koran that Allah changed Jews into apes and pigs (sura 5 verse 60) is to be taken literally, since the Koran is no more or less than the truth itself. "The transformation was actual," we read for example in *Falastin Al-Muslima*, the monthly magazine of Hamas, "as it is not impossible that the omnipotent Allah, who created man in his human form, would not be capable of changing the Jew from human into animal."[197] The only remaining problem confronting Islamic "theoreticians" in this respect is "whether the Jews who were changed into animals had offspring" or whether these strange creatures "lived for no more than three days," since the Koran provides no answer to this question.[198]

Western science, based on doubt and individual cognition, cannot match this God-given "knowledge." On the contrary! Its fatal flaw consists precisely in the fact that it "splits the view of the world," while only the "Islamic *tawhid* (theocentrism) restores the unity of the God-rules cosmos."[199] In this discourse, then, the term "Western imperialism" refers not so much to economic and social aggression, but first and foremost to an "intellectual invasion" of the world of Islam. In the words of the Islamist Syed al-Attas, "The contemporary challenge of Western civilization… is the challenge of knowledge…which promotes scepticism, which has elevated doubt and conjecture to 'scientific status' in its methodology."[200] The primary goal of academic Islamism is to "de-westernise" the sciences, i.e. to free them from the principles of doubt and conjecture.

This explains the intensity of the attacks to which Sadiq al-Asm, a philosopher from Damascus, was subjected in 1969

197. Accoring to Aluma Solnick, Based on Koranic Verses, Interpretations and Traditions, Muslim Clerics Stat: The Jews Are the Descendants of Apes, Pigs, and Other Animal, in: the Special report from MEMRI, November 11, 2002, p. 7.
198. Aluma Solnick, op. cit., p. 8.
199. Tibi 1992, op. cit., p. 108
200. Syed M. N. al-Attas, cited by Tibi 1992, op. cit., p. 139.

on account of his book *Critique of Religious Discourse*. Its asser-
tion that human reason is the source of knowledge, so that "the
scientific method is totally at odds with the religious method,"
led to the book being banned and earned the author a jail term
and the loss of his professorship at the American University in
Beirut. While back in 1969 there was a vociferous public outcry,
twenty years later, according to Bassam Tibi, "such a protest was
no longer conceivable. Islamic fundamentalism has become the
principal feature of public life in the Middle East. Al-Asm's text
became the subject of numerous defamatory writings in Arabic,
which circulate to this day."[201]

This rejection of human reason necessarily affects how power
is understood. The very word Islam means "submission," in the
sense of subjection to God. If people cannot achieve knowledge
through reason, they are even less capable of shaping and deter-
mining their own fate. While the secular answer to the question
"can people rule themselves" is positive, from an Islamist point
of view it is *a priori* negative: only God can rule, only God is the
sovereign. His representative on earth is the Caliph, whose future
rule Islamists consider a certainty. "The Islamic state embodied
in the Caliph...is neither democratic or dictatorial" according
to a statement in *explizit*, an Islamist publication distributed in
Germany. "At no time has the construction of this state...been
'invented' by the Muslims, so that it might be said that this form
of state is not obligatory for us, since it is the product only of fal-
lible human beings. Rather, every one of these institutions has its
origin in an action by the prophet. This state structure is therefore by its nature not a matter of free choice for us, but represents
an Islamic precept which we must follow in this form."[202]

201. Tibi 1992, op. cit., p. 47
202. "Der Aufbau des islamischen Staates," *explizit. Das politisches Magazin
für islamisches Bewußtsein*, no. Nov 29 -Feb. 2001/2, p. 28. *Explizit* was the
organ of the Islamist Hizb ut-Tahrir (Party of Liberation), which was banned
in Germany at the beginning of 2003. See: Anton Maegerle, "Djihad gegen
Juden und Israel," *Tribüne*, Vol. 44, no. 173, p. 185.

The third premise of Islamism is its principle of dominance. The rejection of individual self-determination and critical reason flows from the conviction of already being in possession of a full and self-sufficient body of knowledge. Unlike other tendencies in Islam, therefore, Islamists start from the assumption that their view of the world is destined to prevail over all others. "The Noble Qur'an appoints the Muslims as guardians over humanity," declared Hassan al-Banna, the founder of the Muslim Brothers, "and grants them the right of suzerainty and dominion over the world in order to carry out this sublime commission."[203] Sixty years later Suleiman abu Gheith, the spokesman for al-Qa'ida, in his statement "Why We Fight America," expressed the same idea. How can a Muslim accept all the humiliations, asked Gheith, "when he knows that his nation was created to stand at the center of leadership, at the center of hegemony and rule ....when he knows that the divine rule is that the entire earth must be subject to the religion of Allah?"[204]

The dominance principle defines the proper relationship to all other religious groups and countries. For Islamists, the whole world is divided into two spheres: the *Dar al-Islam* (House of Islam) and the *Dar al-Harb* (House of War), where the unbelievers rule. This straight split is in the best of cases temporarily mitigated by the idea of the *Dar a-Ahd* (House of the Treaty), which allows possible coexistence between the two spheres, but only for a transitional period. So the aim of technological cooperation with the unbelievers of the *Dar al-Harb* is not to perpetuate this coexistence, but, as the Islamist Hasan al-Sharqawi puts it,

203. Hasan Al-Banna, To What Do We Summon Mankind?, in: *Five Tracts of Hasan Al-Banna*, Translated from the Arabic and annotated by Charles Wendell, (Berkely: University of California Press, 1978), p. 71.
204. "'Why We Fight America': Al-Qa'ida Spokesman Explains September 11 and Declares Intention to Kill 4 Million Americans with Weapons of Mass Destruction," *MEMRI, Special Dispatch*, 12 June 2002.

"to learn how to use modern weapons and more than that, to produce and develop them so that we can strike our enemies."[205]

The division of the world into an Islamic and a non-Islamic sphere partially explains the hatred orthodox Muslims feel for Israel: since 1948 the Islamic community has for the first time found itself confronted with the reality of a Jewish state within the *Dar al-Islam*. Many Muslims view the situation in Palestine as a modern version of the early Islamic antagonism between Muhammad and the Jews, with the result that they consider the seventh century expulsion and killing of the Jews as the model for current policy towards Israel. The most radical and at the same time most popular proponent of this jihadist idea is Sayyid Qutb, in whose ideology only two social formations are recognized: the world of Islam and that of barbarism.

Sayyid Qutb

The advance of Islamism since 1967 is inseparable from the dissemination of the writings of the Egyptian Muslim Brother Sayyid Qutb (pronounced Kootup). His writings are read from Morocco to Mindanao and have been translated into almost all the languages of the Islamic world. "Based on my observations of the world of Islam," writes Bassam Tibi, "I can state that militant fundamentalists are far more familiar with Sayyid Qutb's main writings than with the text of the Koran, of which they often know only those parts selectively quoted by Qutb." Given their dissemination and influence, Qutb's writings are "without exaggeration" comparable "to the Communist Manifesto at the time of the early labour movement in Europe."[206]

Sayyid Qutb was born in 1906. His father was a secular nationalist activist. At first, his son followed in his father's foot-

---

205. Tibi, 2000a, op. cit., p.49
206. Tibi 1992, op. cit., pp. 124ff. Tibi 2000a, op. cit., p. 137. Qutb "can be considered the best documented representative of the Egyptian Muslim Brotherhood, if not of the whole Islamist movement," asserts Gudrun Krämer, 1999, op. cit., p. 211.

steps. For 16 years, Qutb worked for the Egyptian Education Ministry and between 1939 and 1947 made a name for himself in particular as a literary critic for the leading Egyptian cultural periodical *al-Risalah*. It was Qutb, for example, who in 1945 discovered the future Nobel Literature Prize winner, Naguib Mahfouz.[207] Only in the 1940s did Qutb turn to the Koran for the first time, partly because of its literary qualities and partly for personal reasons to find consolation and "solid ground." Qutb had particular problems with women. After his adored mother died in 1940, he found solace in an affair and, after that ended, in the Koran.[208] His already pronounced moralism, marked by an aversion to everything "urban," now grew into hatred of every form of "depraved" sensuality. He raged against the "sick singing" on the radio since it undermined the morality and pride of Egypt. He advocated censorship and the establishment of public committees to eliminate this "poison." He was especially horrified by "obscene films," loose morals, and scanty bathing costumes on the beaches of Alexandria. "How I hate and despise this European civilization and eulogize humanity which is being tricked by its luster, noise, and sensual enjoyment in which the soul suffocates and the conscience dies down, while instincts and senses become intoxicated, quarrelsome and excited," he wrote in 1946 in *al-Risalah*.[209]

In 1949 Qutb was sent by his Ministry for a two-and-a-half-year stay in the United States, where his obsessions intensified still further. Immediately after his return in 1951 he joined the Muslim Brotherhood, rising into its leading circle the following year. In this capacity he maintained close contact with Nasser and other representatives of the Free Officers. In 1954 Qutb became editor of the Brotherhood's daily newspaper, although it

207. Adnan Musallam, *Sayyid Qutb, The Emergence of the Islamist 1939-1950* (Jerusalem: Passia Publication, 1997), p. 34 and Barry Rubin, *Islamic Fundamentalism in Egyptian Politics* (London: Macmillan, 1990), p. 49.
208. Musallam, op. cit., pp. 52ff.
209. Musallam, op. cit., p. 60.

was banned after the attempt on Nasser's life in October of that year. In 1955 Qutb was sentenced to 25 years hard labour; he was tortured in prison. Pardoned in 1964 he immediately assumed a leading role in a secret movement for the reorganization of the Brotherhood. After a few months - during which *Signposts*, a book he had written in jail, was published - he was rearrested, charged with high treason, with reference to his book, sentenced to death and in 1966 hanged with two other Muslim Brothers.[210] What are the outstanding features of Qutb's teaching?

While Hassan al-Banna was more of a radical reformer, Sayyid Qutb was the revolutionary. Qutb's writings make pious Muslims into self-confident soldiers, who joyfully devote their lives to the war against Islam's enemies. The purpose of the program is not education or compromise, but a radical rejection of the godless society and an orientation towards Islamic world revolution.

Qutb's message is simple and schematic: human freedom lies in living according to the divine will as embodied in the *sharia*. Justice is what the *sharia* prescribes, while tyranny reigns everywhere that Allah's sovereignty is ignored.[211] Qutb's key idea is therefore that of the *jahiliyya* (state of ignorance). This term denotes the pre-Islamic barbarism and ignorance that is said to have existed before the coming of the prophet to the earth. In Qutb's view, the penetration of western culture had cast Muslim civilization back into the pre-religious barbarism which had reigned among the Bedouin tribes before the coming of Muhammad, characterized by social chaos, sexual licence, polytheism, disbelief and the worship of idols; in short, by arbitrariness instead of religious regulation. Just as Muhammad in his day had to undertake the migration from unbelieving Mecca (known as the *hijra*), in order to return strengthened and able to destroy the

210. Michael Youssef, *Revolt Against Modernity. Muslim Zealots and the West* (Leiden: E.J. Brill, 1985), p. 74 and Kogelmann, op. cit., p. 48.
211. Krämer 1999, op. cit., p. 214.

jahiliyya-society of Mecca, so Qutb now emphasized the need for a new *hijra* as preparation for holy, bloody war. Through declaring them to be party to *jahiliyya*, Qutb accused the rulers of the Islamic world of apostasy, punishable according to Islamic law by death, and one of Qutb's concerns was the carrying out of this penalty.

At the same time, his verdict that the existing world is in *jahiliyya* heralds a liberated and just new world which can only be brought into being by armed struggle and whose promise of bliss seems to justify every martyr's death. For Qutb, the godforsaken state of the world was the final stage before the advent of a charitable and just kingdom of God, the best examples of which to date have been Iran under the Mullahs and Afghanistan under the Taliban.

But whom does Qutb consider to be the adversary of God's rule and the mortal enemy of every believer? Is it the pseudo-Muslim apostates in Cairo, Baghdad or Ankara? Or the representatives of the British and US governments in Egypt? Not at all. Like all modern jihadists, Qutb saw only one eternal adversary. In his 1950 key text *Our Struggle with the Jews* - which was republished in 1970 and distributed throughout the Muslim world by the government of Saudi Arabia - the original Islamic form of Jew-hatred is blended together with the conspiracy-theory side of European antisemitism.[212]

Qutb refers back to the role which the Jews had supposedly played in the conflicts of Islam's early days. "The Jews were enemies of the Muslim Community from the first day," writes Qutb, who goes on, "This bitter war which the Jews launched against Islam ... is a war, which has not been extinguished, even for one moment, for close on fourteen centuries, and which continues until this moment, its blaze raging in all corners of the earth."

212. Qutb's essay is reproduced in full in: Ronald L. Nettler, *Past Trials and Present Tribulations: A Muslim Fundamentalist's View of the Jews* (Oxford: Pergamon Press, 1987), pp. 72-87.

At the same time, the delusion of the Jewish world conspiracy is recycled in lurid tones. "Jews in the latest era" have become "the chiefs of the struggle with Islam, on every foot of the face of the earth," he claims. "The Jews also utilize Christianity and idolatry in this comprehensive war.... They attack every foundation of this religion in a Crusader-Zionist war!!" In Qutb's eyes, the Jews are to blame for everything they have suffered over the centuries, and this applies to Hitler and the Shoah too. Thus, in the modern period, "the Jews again returned to evil-doing and consequently Allah ... brought Hitler to rule over them." But even the "punishment" meted out by Hitler was not sufficiently terrible, since "once again today the Jews have returned to evil-doing, in the form of 'Israel'. ... So let Allah bring down upon the Jewish people ... the worst kind of punishment." Qutb's message is internally consistent: the Jew is the source of evil in the world, the Shoah is therefore no crime and Israel deserves to be erased from the map. Demonization of the Jews, legitimization of the Holocaust, and liquidation of Israel: three sides of an ideological triangle that cannot exist if any one of the sides is missing.

Was Qutb's antisemitism a response to the foundation of Israel shortly before this essay was written? Not at all. The target of his hatred of "the Jews" is the threatening side of modernity, with which he identifies them.

In Qutb's fantasyland, not only is everything Jewish evil, but everything evil is Jewish. Particularly evil for him, however, are sexuality and sensuality. Alluding to Karl Marx, Sigmund Freud and Emile Durkheim, Qutb writes: "Behind the doctrine of atheistic materialism was a Jew; behind the doctrine of animalistic sexuality was a Jew; and behind the destruction of the family and the shattering of the sacred relationship in society ... was a Jew.... They free the sensual desires from their restraints and they destroy the moral foundation on which the pure Creed rests, in order that the Creed should fall into the filth which they spread so widely on this earth."

Muslim leaders who deviate even slightly from the pure teaching of the *sharia* and the Koran are regarded with special loathing. For objective reasons, in Qutb's view, such creatures can only be one thing: Zionist agents. "The Tens of personalities who have been foisted upon the Muslim Community (as conspirators against it) in the guise of 'heroes' were manufactured by Zionism, in order that these 'heroes' should do for the enemies of Islam what these enemies are themselves not able to do openly ... Anyone who leads this Community away from its Religion and its Qur'an can only be a Jewish agent – whether he does this wittingly or unwittingly, willingly or unwillingly."

If these "agents" acted in ways contrary to Qutb's assumptions, then this was clearly an especially devious form of trickery. Not only are the Jews "deceiving it [the Islamic community] about the reality of its enemies and their ultimate goals," but also their public manner is marked by malicious deceit. "The agents of Zionism today ... agree with each other on ... the destruction of this (Islamic) Creed at the first auspicious and unrepeatable opportunity. This Jewish consensus would never be found in a pact or open conference. Rather it is the (secret) agreement of one [Zionist] agent with another on this important goal."

Like his theories about *jahiliyya*, Qutb's exuberant Jew-hatred and his view of Adolf Hitler as a man sent by God to chastise the Jews have had a decisive influence on the thought and actions of later Islamist movements. The jihad advocated by al-Banna and the early Muslim Brothers focused on the Zionist project in Palestine. The jihadist movement of the 1980s followed Qutb's approach and found its targets in Egypt itself.

Jihad against the Muslims

In 1977 Egyptian President Anwar as-Sadat unexpectedly broke ranks. On November 19, he became the first Arab politician to address the Knesset, the Israeli Parliament. Subsequent talks at Camp David led in 1979 to a peace treaty between Egypt and

Israel. Israel now did what it had offered to do in the case of a normalization of relations; it withdrew from the Sinai Peninsula that accounted for 90% of the territory occupied in 1967.[213]

Two years later, peace with Israel cost Sadat his life. On October 6, 1981 he was shot by a commando unit of the Egyptian *Tanzim al-Jihad* organization. The assassination was meant to be the opening shot in an Islamic revolution. In Cairo *al-Jihad* attempted to seize control of the radio and TV stations. Security service premises were attacked and Cairo airport occupied.[214] The attempted uprising had been preceded by a furious anti-Sadat campaign by the Muslim Brothers, in which peace with Israel was declared incompatible with Koranic precepts. Moreover, in Qutb-like tones, the peace treaty was demonized as a Jewish plot against Islam, with Sadat in the role of the Zionist agent.[215] In spite of a strict ban on demonstrations, pro-Islamist students took to the streets in Alexandria and Assiut chanting "no peace with Israel," while the Brotherhood's mass circulation paper, *al-Daawa*, under the headline "It is impossible to live in peace with the Jews," recounted Muhammad's anti-Jewish campaigns of the seventh century.[216]

Tanzim al-Jihad, while ideologically close to the Muslim Brothers, was not organizationally linked to them. Many members of the Brotherhood had reached middle age and formed a significant part of the Egyptian bourgeoisie. Their relationship with the new militant jihadi organizations was ambivalent. They still considered themselves part of the Islamist and anti-Zionist

213.   Sadat's new course resulted from Egypt's utterly bleak economic situation, which had left the country totally dependent on the USA and rendered impossible the further growth in the defence budget required to win the Sinai Peninsula by war. The political background to Sadat's initiative is described in David Kimche, *The Last Option. After Nasser, Arafat and Saddam Hussein* (London: Weidenfeld and Nicolson, 1991), pp. 44-87.
214.   Serauky, op. cit., pp. 57ff.
215.   Kogelmann, op. cit., p. 104 and Nettler, op. cit., p. 105.
216.   Hiro, op. cit., p. 76.

movement, but rejected attacks on Egyptian leaders and Qutb's *jahiliyya* doctrine.

The *al-Jihad* group, on the other hand, with 5,000-10,000 members and hundreds of thousands of sympathisers in 1980, was young and rebellious. The group's founder, the engineer Abd as-Salam Farag, whose father had been jailed several times for membership in the Muslim Brotherhood[217], was known in particular as the author of the manifesto *al-Jihad al-Farida al-Ga'iba* ("Jihad, the Absent Religious Duty") which had appeared at the start of the 1980s and gave Qutb's doctrine an even more radical twist. The main reason for all the humiliations suffered by the Islamic world was deemed to be the renunciation of jihad and attachment to the "comforts of life in this world" although these "are small in comparison with the comforts of the next." In order to end this situation, the military form of jihad must be regarded as the sixth duty of all Muslims and extended in an ongoing campaign into the realm of the unbelievers.[218] Referring to Qutb's *jahiliyya* concept, Farag stressed that Israel and imperialism only existed because corrupt Muslim leaders allowed them to. The war against the "near enemy" - the apostate Muslim leaders - must therefore have priority over that against the "far enemy."[219]

Farag's concept of revolution brought him great success, especially in the universities. 45% of the *al-Jihad* members arrested after the attempted revolt in 1981 were students; 43% were between 20 and 25-years old. The majority of this student generation had come from the rural areas to the cities where they were especially sharply confronted with the worsening social problems - inflation, horrendous housing costs, the juxtaposition of mass poverty and immense wealth and their own lack

217. Youssef, op. cit., p. 124 and Kogelmann pp. 134ff and 131.
218. The other five obligations of all Muslims are the Islamic creed, fasting in Ramadan, praying five times a day after ritual washing, distribution of alms to the poor and pilgrimage to Mecca.
219. Farag's manifesto is reproduced almost in full in Youssef, op. cit., p. 146ff.

of career prospects. Jihad offered the promise of escape from this misery. It held out the possibility of wielding power over unbelievers or attaining paradise through martyrdom. Michael Youssef, investigating this group in his study *Revolt against Modernity* notes that, although *al-Jihad* was in no way established on Marxist foundations, "However, as one spends hours listening to members bitterly attacking the 'rich' an the 'corrupt', it is impossible to ignore that the spirit of Marxism in its revolutionary fervor is very much evident in the heart and the soul of the movement."[220]

Here, Youssef falls prey to an error typical of many observers and sympathisers of Islamism. He fails to see that "revolutionary energy" need not have anything to do with a striving for emancipation. He ignores the fact that mass movements can also be mobilized behind fascist revolutionary programs. A revolutionary "anti-capitalist" and antisemitic consciousness was certainly a constitutive element of the Nazi mass movements.[221]

The idealization of mass movements whose "anti-capitalism" is fuelled by the antisemitic mindset ought therefore to be excluded. But precisely the opposite is the case. Rather than give up their fantasies about the inherent innocence and progressiveness of the "masses," many present and former leftwingers seem to wish to join antisemitic mass movements. "Why," asks the scholar of Islamism Gilles Keppel, "have so many former Marxists throughout the Islamic world committed themselves to the Islamist cause?" Because they are guided by the conviction, that, "given that 'the masses' have joined this movement, the task is to emphasise its 'progressive' and popular character, so as to transform the Islamist movement into an anti-imperi-

---

220. Youssef, op. cit., pp. 119 and 135.
221. Ulrike Becker, Matthias Küntzel et al., *Goldhagen und die deutsche Linke* (Berlin, Elefanten Press, 1997), p. 157. Here can be found (pp. 85ff) a more detailed examination of the Nazis' anti-capitalism, in which "the Jews" personify the abstract side of capitalism.

alist and anti-capitalist one."[222] But the "anti-imperialism" and "anti-capitalism" of the Islamists have never had a progressive meaning. They have constantly used terroristic means to combat endeavors for individual and social self-consciousness, considered tantamount to apostasy.

For example, Assiut, Egypt's third biggest city with 200,000 inhabitants, became an *al-Jihad* stronghold. Here the organization's patrols forced unmarried men and women to walk on opposite sides of the street. Women whom *al-Jihad* considered to be incorrectly dressed were aggressively abused and, if they argued, physically assaulted. Vendors of alcohol who did not close up shop were beaten to death. The owner of a shoe shop who played music loudly on his radio, but turned it down when prayers came on, was imprisoned for forty days because, the police explained, he would otherwise have been killed by the *al-Jihadi* gangs. In 1981 *al-Jihad* had in reality more influence in Assiut than the city council or police. As a local police chief later stated, it had been none other than Sadat who had allowed this kind of dual power. "We had government orders that we should not stop them or interfere with their activities."[223]

Assiut has remained a bastion of Islamist terror under Sadat's successor Hosni Mubarak. In 1992, in battles between Islamists and the state apparatus, not only 84 policemen but also 14 members of the Coptic Christian minority were killed. The Copts were murdered for one reason only: as a minority, they were cast in the role that the antisemitic mindset normally reserves for the Jews. Thus some Copts had entered the middle classes, benefiting from the well-developed Christian school system. The Islamists considered it a scandal that Christians, who in their eyes should live in humble modesty, should display their prosperity while Muslims suffered. Islamist leaflets therefore depicted "the Christian as a perverse being, who shamelessly exploits his unjustified

222. Kepel, op. cit., p. 89.
223. Youssef, op. cit., pp. 102 and 95.

social superiority." In other statements they were pilloried as "foreign agents or crusaders, constantly seeking to corrupt Muslims."[224] There were an increasing number of terror attacks on Copts. "Bone-breaking in order to maim them, attacks on Coptic schools so that they had to be placed under police protection and sieges of the churches to which many Copts fled were the terrorists' favourite methods there. The aim was to force the Copts to leave the country immediately."[225] In Assiut, the use of terror to control "unbelieving" Muslims was combined with projective hatred of the Copts: needs which the jihadis denied in themselves were projected onto and attributed to the Copts who could then be punished for them. The terroristic unified community necessarily requires the exclusion of those stigmatized as the "Other."

For our second example, let us take a closer look at an Islamist project of the 1980s from Cairo's Embaba district. Here we see the connection between poverty and Islamist indoctrination in a nutshell. In 1984 the Islamist *gamaʿa al-islamiyya* (Islamic community) embarked on the systematic infiltration of this urban district with a million inhabitants in order to transform it into an Islamized zone.[226] This slum area on the city's outskirts was marked by unbearable social evils: lack of electrification, disastrous sanitary conditions, 42% of men, 57% of women and 49% of children over ten illiterate, 21% of the children under 14 working as unskilled labour and a child mortality rate of 75%. Fertile ground then for the agitation of the Islamists, who established a genuine social security apparatus delivering all those social services that the Egyptian state was either unwilling or unable to provide. But here too the social carrot was accompanied by the jihadi stick. While the *gamaʿa* provided school-age orphans with

224. Kepel, op. cit., p. 342.
225. Serauky, op. cit., p. 117.
226. From the *gamaʿat al-islamiyya* (plural), which brought various Islamist currents together in the 1970s, there emerged in the 1980s the tightly organized *gamaʿa al-islamiyya* (singular) led by Sheikh Omar Abdel Rahman.

school equipment and clothes, music and theatre were strictly forbidden. While they established advice centres for family-law issues, unveiled women were threatened with the most brutal physical punishments. While they founded Islamist businesses, they banned all sales of videos and small shops that defied them were levelled to the ground. In Embaba too the Copts, who had 21 churches, were especially hard hit. Since there were no Jews on whom the Islamists could vent their conformist rage, Coptic shops were plundered and their churches set ablaze.

However, when in 1992 the *gama'a* informed an international press agency that an Islamic state based on the *sharia* had arisen in Embaba, enough was enough: the Egyptian state struck back. In December 1992 14,000 police officers occupied the district for a week, making 5,000 arrests. Considerable sums were allocated for reconstruction, including the establishment of a socio-political infrastructure.[227] But even these measures could not stop the forward march of Islamism, as the following chapter shows.

Islamization under Mubarak

In July 1997 the *gama'a* leadership drew conclusions from their failed offensive strategy and called a ceasefire. By this time 34,000 of its members were in jail and some 1,000 had died in various police operations.[228] The terror wave of the past year had petered out. The scale of this civil war was rarely truly grasped in the West. In 1993, 207 people died in clashes between Islamists and the Egyptian state, among them 90 police officers, six Copts, three tourists, 39 passers-by and 69 Islamists. In 1994, the death toll was 279, including 94 police officers. In 1995, the number rose to 453, a 60% rise over the previous year.[229]

The state did not respond with kid gloves. In the space of 17 months, from December 1992 to April 1994, Mubarak had

227. On Embaba, see Kepel, op. cit., pp. 345ff and Serauky, op. cit., pp. 92ff.
228. Kepel, op. cit., p. 354 and Serauky, op. cit., p. 152.
229. Serauky, op. cit., pp. 128, 131 and 152.

sentences handed out under Nasser is enlightening. Under his rule a total of nine death sentences were carried out in the eighteen years between 1952 and 1970.

However, it was not this repression that the *gamaʾa* gave as the reason for their change of course. As their lawyer Muntassir az-Zayyat explained, the *gamaʾa* had not changed its approach, but its goal. "Within the *gamaʾa*, it has been realized that the real enemy is not the Egyptian government, but Israel." The *gamaʾa* leadership was ashamed "that it had fought against the excessively low neckline of an actress, while other groups such as Hizbullah and Hamas risked their lives for the liberation of their country." [230] The Islamist strategy shifted anew. From the struggle against the "near enemy" prioritized by Qutb and Farag, the main struggle would now be against the "far enemy" i.e. Israel. In line with this, the strategy of terror against "corrupted Muslims" was replaced by that of Islamist infiltration of the institutions.

This infiltration had in practice already been under way for years. Only three years after Sadat's murder the Islamists dominated all the essential sectors of society. By 1984 they were once again the strongest force in the universities. In addition, elections for the governing committees of Egypt's 22 professional associations went almost entirely in their favor.[231]

Almost inexorably, Islamism gained ground in the state institutions too. In 1984 the *sharia*'s status as the basis of law was further reinforced. The Egyptian Parliament repealed a legal provision established by Sadat (under the influence of his wife Jihan) according to which a husband, despite the basic acceptance of polygamy, had to ask permission from his first wife before taking a second.[232] In 1985 all television programs which

---

230. "Abschied vom Djihad. Kehrtwende von Ägyptens Jamaa al-islamiyya," *Neue Züricher Zeitung*, March 27, 2002. 100,000 copies of the four books justifying the new course written behind bars by the *gamaʾa*'s founders were sold within a few weeks.
231. Kepel, op. cit., p. 342.
232. Serauky, op. cit., p. 68.

were "incompatible with Islamic values," for example programs about dancing, including classical European ballet, were prohibited. At the same time, 14,000 hours a year were reserved for religious broadcasting. In this way the hegemonic influence of the "Telekoran" preachers, often close to the Muslim Brotherhood, was secured.[233]

At the same time, the Islamists were ready to go beyond legal means to intimidate the remaining secularist intellectuals, murdering their most prominent representative, Farag Foda, in 1992. Foda was one of the few who had vehemently and publicly called for Egypt to establish normal relations with Israel. His murder was explicitly supported by a figure from the semi-official Al-Azhar mosque, the Muslim Brother Sheikh Muhammad al-Ghazzali. According to al-Ghazzali, anyone born a Muslim who fights against *sharia* deserves the death penalty. Since an Islamic state able to uphold the law does not yet exist, those who carried out the sentence cannot be evil.[234] Another victim was Nasr Hamid Abu Zaid, Professor of Linguistics, who was declared an "apostate" and forcibly divorced from his wife by a Supreme Court decision, since - according to the judgment - an apostate cannot be married to a Muslim woman. As the death threats multiplied, the couple were forced to flee to Europe. In October 1994 even the Nobel Literature prize-winner Naguib Mahfouz was seriously wounded in a murder attempt by a member of the *gamaʿa*. As Yusif al-Badri, a Cairo Imam, explained, Mahfouz, through the heretical symbolism of his books, had shown that he had abandoned the faith.[235] The most recent prominent victim is 63-year-old Saad Eddin Ibrahim, an internationally renowned sociologist, who was sentenced in August 2002 to seven years hard labour on the ludicrous grounds that he had received EU

233. Kepel, op. cit., p. 336.
234. Kepel, op. cit., pp. 342ff and Serauky, op. cit., pp.112ff.
235. Tibi 2000a, op. cit., p. 105.

research grants.[236] Such legal and extra-legal assaults not only contribute to the Islamists' advance in Egypt, but also serve the immediate interests of the existing regime. Hosni Mubarak has never lifted the state of emergency declared in 1981 following Sadat's murder. He was presumably happy to know that his critic Ibrahim was breaking rocks. Following a threat from President Bush to freeze American financial aid to Egypt in August 2002, Ibrahim was released in March 2003.[237]

However, it is not the secular intellectuals who are identified as the real "evil" responsible for all Egypt's troubles, but Israel and the Jews. On this point, the entire Egyptian society has been islamized. In Egypt the ostracism and demonization of Jews is not a matter of debate, but a basic assumption of everyday discourse. As if the Egyptian-Israeli peace treaty had never been signed, Israel and Israelis are today totally boycotted by every Egyptian professional organization - be it lawyers, journalists, doctors or artists - and by all Egyptian universities, sports associations, theatres and orchestras. When in 1995 the Syrian poet Adonis attended a conference with Israeli colleagues, every political current in Egypt attacked him. In the case of Farag Foda, because he had spoken out in favor of Egyptian-Israeli reconciliation, the nationalist left joined in the applause for his murder.[238] If there is one theme in contemporary Egypt which unites Islamists, Liberals, Nasserites and Marxists, it is the collective fantasy of the common enemy in the shape of Israel and the Jews, which almost always correlates with the wish to destroy Israel.

How unremarkable it is even today for Hitler-style antisemitism to imbue an Egyptian religious textbook is demonstrated by the standard text, *"The people of Israel in the Koran and Sunna"* by Sheikh Muhammad Sayed Tantawi. Tantawi

236. Thomas L. Friedman, "Shame on Washington," *IHT*, August 5, 2002. S. E. Ibrahim is among other things, author of *Egypt, Islam and Democracy* (Cairo, 1996).
237. See *FAZ*, August 16, 2002 and *NZZ*, March 19, 2003.
238. Kepel, op. cit., p. 342.

is the Head of Cairo's Al-Azhar University, which means he is one of Sunni Islam's most renowned spiritual authorities. The fourth edition of his book - it was also his PhD thesis, written in 1967 - appeared in 1997. In it, Tantawi writes that the Jews were behind the French and October Revolutions. That they provoked the First and Second World Wars. That they control the world's media and economy. That they endeavor to destroy morality and religion and run brothels worldwide. Tantawi, the highest Sunni Muslim theologian, quotes Adolf Hitler's remark in *Mein Kampf* that "in resisting the Jew, I am doing the work of the Lord." He praises the *Protocols of the Elders of Zion*, noting without the slightest trace of sympathy that "after the publication of the Protocols in Russia, some 10,000 Jews were killed."[239]

The same ideas appear in non-religious guise in Muhammad Qutb's *Muslims and Globalization*, which appeared in 2000. Behind globalization, according to Qutb, lies "international Jewish capital, which already controls its lands of origin and is now striving to extend that rule across the whole world." To this end, it employs a particularly perfidious strategy, since the "history of Jewish power over people" is expressed through "the dissemination of moral depravity, sexual anarchy, heresy, drugs and different forms of madness and obsession."[240]

Anyone who believes in such notions is bound, as an inhabitant of a country bordering on Israel, to feel a sense of permanent and especially sinister threat. Remarkably often this threat is embodied in the Israeli woman.

Just as the 9/11 bomber Muhammad Atta stipulated in his will that, in the event of his demise, no woman should touch his body, so mainstream Egyptian media present the very touch of a female Jew as a diabolic threat. Egyptian street-stalls offer a

---

239. Wolfgang Driesch, *Islam, Judentum und Israel*, Deutsches Orient-Institut, Mitteilungen Band 66 (Hamburg, 2003), pp. 76ff. The Hitler quotation is from *Mein Kampf* (Munich: Franz Eher Nachfolger, 1934), p. 70.
240. Nordbruch, op. cit.

a female Jew as a diabolic threat. Egyptian street-stalls offer a host of books in which prostitutes allegedly working for Mossad launch the most perfidious assaults on Egypt's young men. These Sirens are not only advancing a cunning plan to bring about the normalization of relations with Israel, by undermining the natural Arab forces of resistance through sex, but are pursuing the direct destruction of the Arab population by deliberately and systematically spreading AIDS.[241]

Egypt felt itself threatened by a "sexual invasion" of a very special kind when the trans-sexual Israeli-Arab Dana International won the Eurovision song contest for Israel and her Arab songs found an audience among young Egyptians. "Thus Israel tries to destroy us by any means," warned one Egyptian newspaper. "Will she succeed, or will our youths establish that they are really Egyptian?"[242]

As a deterrent, an anti-Dana book was published exposing her popularity as a "Masonic-Jewish conspiracy" because Dana was promoting the individual rights to happiness and sensual pleasure and thus those very principles which the Freemasons and Jews had first invented in order to destroy society.[243] As a precaution, all Dana International tapes were banned and the number of police raids on music shops stepped up.

Such preventive measures are signs of the attraction exerted by a less restrictive sexual morality on young people whose possibilities of sexual expression are blocked in two directions: firstly through the extremely strict *sharia*-based punishment of any premarital sexual relations and secondly through the fact that the social code dictates that men can only marry (in itself

241. See Götz Nordbruch, *Holocaustleugnung und Antisemitismus in der arabischen Welt*, unpublished manuscript, 2002.
242. Ted Swedenburg, "Sa'ida Sultan/Dana International: Transgender Pop and the Polysemiotics of Sex, Nation and Ethnicity on the Israeli-Egyptian Border," in Walter Armbrust (ed.), *Mass Mediations. New Approaches to Popular Culture in the Middle East and Beyond* (San Francisco: The University of California Press, 2000), Internet version, p. 20.
243. Swedenburg, op. cit., p. 3.

household, something of which many Egyptian university and high-school graduates can only dream.

Once again we see the important role played in the antisemitic mentality by the projection mechanism which casts the individual desire for sexual and sensual pleasure into the outside world, projects it onto Israel and seeks to destroy it there.

The sexual self-denial that underlies this projection results from the "religious anxiety" (Wilhelm Reich) systematically agitated by Islamism. This brings us back to our original question: why is Islamism still dominant in Egypt today?

This much at least is clear: Egypt, which, with al-Banna and his Muslim Brothers, first brought modern jihadism into the world, has remained the centre of Sunni Islamism for the past fifty years. Admittedly, in the periods following the attempted assassination of Nasser (1956-1967) and the successful one of Sadat (1981-1984), its activists could only operate clandestinely and behind prison walls. In the remaining postwar periods, however, Islamism has made constant ideological and political progress.

Were the impoverished masses driven into the Islamists' arms by material hardship? The connection between poverty and Islamism is more complicated than the schema of cause and effect suggests: the radicalization of Islam is less a consequence of poverty and lack of opportunity than its cause.

Islamists consider bending down so low that one's head touches the dust a sign of spirituality, while they denounce the striving for individual development, prosperity and riches as trivial and unimportant. Islamism entails individual self-impoverishment and the extinction of such possibilities for development as may exist even under adverse conditions.

At the same time under-development fosters tendencies towards radical Islam since the Koran offers even the poorest believer the consolation of ruling over women and permission to take part in religious purges. The under-development of whole regions of the world offers the Islamists ever new recruiting grounds, since it fosters the disintegration of states and the collapse of public education and health systems. In this sense a connection does exist between the success of Islamism and capitalism insofar as the latter creates poverty in many parts of the world. Under-development, however, is often exacerbated by questionable political priorities, as well. Since, for example, Pakistan prefers to invest its meagre budget in the "Islamic bomb" rather than public education, Saudi-financed religious fanatics have stepped into the vacuum, setting up thousands of Koranic schools which offer the young people placed in their charge food and shelter.

In Egypt, the strength of Islam has even less to do with the logic of capitalism. Firstly, economic developments in the Arab world are often politically determined: without their politically motivated boycott of Israel, the Arab world would find itself better off economically. Secondly, at the start of the 1990s Egypt was doing far better economically than, for example, Poland, South Africa or Turkey. From 1989 onwards, at a time when Islamism was achieving new heights of success, the Egyptian economy "grew at an impressive rate. Then in 1999 a downturn set in."[244] If poverty may be conducive to the spread of Islamism, it is evidently not its root cause nor is the creation of prosperity an antidote.

It would be truer to say that Egyptian Islamism is the result of a specific state policy. Thus Sadat maintained and intensified the religious turn initiated by his predecessor until he himself fell victim to the movement he had sponsored. The seeds he sowed in the universities in the 1970s truly burst forth under Mubarak. Both presidents used Islamism to strengthen their own power. So was Egyptian Islamism deliberately created by the state for the purposes of ideologically manipulating potentially insur-

244. Rainer Hermann, "Der 11. September legt die Versäumnisse der Wirtschaftspolitik offen," *FAZ*, February 11, 2002, and Serauky, op. cit., p. 15.

gent masses? This theory too misses the mark. At the outset, no outside force financed Hassan al-Banna's Muslim Brotherhood, which nonetheless grew into a mass movement. In particular, the martyrdom cult demonstrates the deadly seriousness with which the Islamic war is conducted for its own sake. We are not dealing here with mercenaries enrolling in a cause that is not their own. It is therefore hardly surprising that all those who have hoped to use Islamism for their own ends have been taught a lesson. Among them are the USA, which armed Osama bin Laden in order to defeat the USSR, Israel, which tolerated Hamas to undermine the PLO, and Sadat, who wanted to stabilize his rule with the help of the *gama'a*, and in so doing dug his own grave.

Instead, the strength of Egyptian Islamism rests on a specific historical development that correlates with its Manichean worldview. To the radical social and cultural changes provoked by the advance of modernity, Islamism reacts with a system of ideas which reads everything that happens according to a binary logic: everywhere, the embattled "good" (Islam) is engaged in an existential struggle with "evil." There is, therefore, only one choice: either one's own destruction or annihilation of the evil. The fantasy of an extremely threatening and essentially "evil" opponent is a prerequisite for molding one's own group (the "good") into an inherently harmonious "us." So, "they" are "our" misfortune and everything would be great with "us," if "they" did not exist.[245]

Only this concept of the enemy could give the Islamists what they most ardently sought: an apparently homogeneous community providing a firm sense of security and a secure identity.

Zionist immigration into Palestine and the founding of the State of Israel provided Egyptian Islamism with a suitable enemy and thus provided the most important prerequisite for its

---

245. Thomas Haury, "Der Antizionismus der Neuen Linken in der BRD," in Arbeitskreis Kritik des deutschen Antisemitismus (ed.), *Antisemitismus - die deutsche Normalität, Geschichte und Wirkungsweise des Vernichtungswahns* (Freiburg: Ca ira, 2001), p. 218.

formation. Not because Zionism and its state-building project presented a real threat to the Egyptian people, but because the obsession with Zionism and Israel played and continues to play a functional role in welding together the Islamic community in an imaginary defensive struggle.

This proposition is at odds with the widely held view that Arab hatred of Jews was or is nourished primarily by concrete experiences with Zionism or Israeli policies. Instead, it assumes, that Islamists will be sure to find their obsession confirmed by whatever Zionism or the Israeli government does or does not do.

Thus, actual Zionist actions have never really been relevant to the Muslim Brothers and the Mufti's Jew-hatred. To this day, Islamists remain wholly indifferent to the real Israel. They do not want to influence its government and its people by political action. Only in fantasized form, as the embodiment of pure evil, does the Jewish state serve the function ascribed to it.

Why was a colonial power such as Britain not chosen to play this role? Firstly, the conflict with Britain lacked religious symbolism. That country was not interested in specific holy places nor did it demand its own state in the Middle East. Secondly, the British were too strong for their existence to be challenged. This strength, moreover, allowed them a certain degree of flexibility in their dealings with the Arab states. Britain was therefore unsuited to the role of a unifying hate object.

Israel and the Jews, on the other hand, were far better qualified for the job. Firstly, there was the central Muslim symbol of Jerusalem. Secondly, the whole of the former Ottoman Empire was considered part of the "House of Islam." In the orthodox Muslim view, the establishment of a Jewish state inside the *Dar al-Islam* called for war. Thirdly, in a Jew versus Muslim scenario, memories of Muhammad's battles with the Jews of Medina could be summoned up. The direct carrying over of seventh century Bedouin religious struggles to the present day may seem crazy to secular minds, but orthodox Muslims consider it a religious imperative. Fourthly, the Koranic statement that the Jews are the believers' worst foe helped in their designation as the ultimate enemy.

This form of Islamist demonization was in no way objectively predetermined by religion, as the case of the Tunisian President Habib Bourguiba shows. Not only did he come out at an early stage in favor of the recognition of Israel, he also interpreted the Koranic position on women in an entirely different way to the Muslim Brothers. In 1957 he banned polygamy, giving religious grounds, ensured women equal rights in divorce cases and guaranteed every women whether married or not the right to free abortion in the first three months of pregnancy.[246] Bourguiba showed that both in relation to women and Israel a very different approach to that of the Islamists was possible within an Islamic framework. Might not the Jewish immigration of the first third of the last century have been used as an opportunity for regional development, and the self-confident Jewish presence in the *Dar al-Islam* as a spur to the abandonment of the long-outmoded Islamic assumption of dominance?

At this point, the role and significance of European Fascism and above all of German National Socialism, whose defining feature was exterminatory antisemitism, come into play. In the 1930s it threw its weight behind the Islamists and thus contributed to the fact that it was not the reform course embarked on by Bourguiba or Atatürk, but the identity-molding message that "the Jew is our misfortune" which got the upper hand. The Mufti of Jerusalem acted in the British mandate territory like a local henchman of the Nazis. Hitler's agents fuelled the Muslim Brothers' anti-Zionist struggle in Palestine with money and slogans and this in turn fostered their progress in Egypt. Islamism remains marked by this connection to this day.

246. Minai, op. cit., pp. 80ff.

The Mufti's successful rehabilitation in 1946 entailed the rehabilitation of Nazism and its anti-Zionist and antisemitic outlook. The fascination exerted on the Arab intelligentsia by the *Protocols of the Elders of Zion* ever since then is connected to this rehabilitation. Through the dissemination of the *Protocols*, the obsessive wish to destroy the Jewish state is awakened anew in each generation. The refusal to this day to reflect critically on the Mufti's pro-Nazi activity and the Muslim Brothers' pro-Mufti activity is intimately linked to the Arabic media's coverage of the Holocaust. "If you had only done it, my brother" was the *Al-Akhbar* commentator's complaint to his German idol Adolf Hitler. This appeal is a clear sign of the Mufti's posthumous victory. "If you had only done it." In reality there were now other forces ready "to do it." Jews were being murdered almost daily further to the east, in Tel Aviv and Netanja.

CHAPTER THREE

. . . .

THE JIHAD OF HAMAS

"Thousands of demonstrators took to the streets, shouting 'Allahu Akbar' (God is Great), 'down with Communism', 'long live Islam.' During the demonstration the ... militants attacked cafes, video shops and liquor stores. ... Two days later the offices of the secular *al-Quds* newspaper were set on fire, and a cinema, billiard hall and bar in Gaza were closed."

Where was this scene played out? In Cairo in 1948? In Assiut in 1988? Not at all. These events took place in 1980 in the Israeli-occupied Gaza strip. The protagonists were members of the *Mujama al-Islami* (Islamic Congress), from which, when the intifada began in 1987, the Islamic Resistance Movement (*Harakat al-Muqawama al-Islamiyya*) usually known by its abbreviation, Hamas, emerged. Hamas takes as its reference point the Muslim Brotherhood, and defines itself as the Brotherhood's Palestinian branch. Sheikh Ahmed Yasin, the founder of the *Mujama* and Hamas, had the same significance for the Palestinian movement as Hassan al-Banna had for the original Muslim Brothers.

Born in 1936 in the Mandate Territory, Yasin very early on came into contact with the Egyptian Muslim Brothers, who controlled the school and mosque in his village. In 1948 his family fled to the Gaza strip. He joined the Brotherhood in 1955 and in 1973 founded the *Mujama*. In its first years of existence, this organization built up a solid base of support through social and educational work. It set up small clinics, dental practices, kindergartens, sports facilities and Koranic schools. Saudi Arabia,

Kuwait and Jordan financed these activities. The organization did not publish texts of its own, distributing instead the writings of al-Banna and Qutb. "We have to be patient," declared Yasin, who adopted al-Banna's approach in this respect too, "because Islam will spread sooner or later and will have control all over the world. Patience will shorten the journey of Islam."[247] Once they had created a mass base through their welfare activities, the *Mujama* embarked on the second stage of their policy.

Islamist terror in Gaza

At this point, the *Mujama* showed little interest in Zionism and the Israeli occupation. They saw the Palestinian left and secular nationalism as their main enemies and from 1980 onwards waged a systematic campaign against them. The most important battlefield was Islamic University of Gaza, which, with 4,500 students, was the largest in the occupied territories in the mid-1980s. The *Mujama* systematically turned this university into an Islamist training ground. Small weapons dumps were located in campus cellars. Students and teachers failing to abide by orthodox Islamic practices were assaulted by armed gangs. Among the first victims were beardless men and women not wearing the veil (*hijab*) or the body-enveloping garment known as the *thobe*. Next, students were identified and punished for "unislamic behavior" as "drug-dealers" and "prostitutes."[248] At the same time all teaching content was rigorously islamized.

In contemporary interviews Hamas leaders like to refer to the achievements of this training centre. "We are not in any way superstitious people," Hamas leader Mahmoud al-Zahar, for

247. Beverley Milton-Edwards, *Islamic Politics in Palestine* (London: Tauris Academic Studies, 1996), p. 100. The following remarks are based on her account. The quotation at the start of this chapter is taken from pp. 107ff of this book.
248. "Ziad Abu-Amr, Shaykh Ahmad Yasin and the Origins of Hamas" in R. Scott Appleby (ed.), *Spokesmen for the Despized. Fundamentalist Leaders of the Middle East* (Chicago: University of Chicago Press, 1997), p. 239.

example, asserted in an interview with the *Süddeutsche Zeitung*. "We are doctors, engineers. The best-educated people are in Hamas. We don't live with myths. We have the highest academic level in this society."[249]

But what is the substance of this "highest educational level"? In her study *Islamic Politics in Palestine* Beverley Milton-Edwards recounts the exemplary fate of a student called Bassam, a sympathizer of the left-nationalist People's Front for the Liberation of Palestine (PFLP). In a seminar, Bassam's professor explained that Darwin's theory of natural selection was of Jewish origin: only the Jews could have induced Darwin to link the appearance of humanity with the development of apes. Since, according to the Koran, God created human beings, Islamists have no choice but to regard the theory of evolution as false. Bassam, however, not being an Islamist, dared openly to contradict his teacher. With disastrous consequences. After his interruption, he was repeatedly beaten up. His family were incited against the "atheist." He was subjected to an acid attack. Finally, Bassam saved his own life by giving in to the Islamists and submitting to the prayer rituals in the mosques.[250]

To this day, it seems virtually impossible to graduate from Gaza's Islamic University without becoming an anti-Semite. "Lies have been revealed about murdered Jews and the Holocaust," declared Dr. Issam Sissalem, a history professor at the University, in a broadcast on a Palestinian Authority television channel in November 2000. "Of course, all this is lies and unjustified assertions. No Chelmno, no Dachau, no Auschwitz! This was about disinfection facilities." On the same channel the University's former Director, Dr Ahmad Abu Halabiya, called for a massacre: "Show the Jews no mercy, regardless of where they are, regardless of which country. When you meet them, kill them. Wherever you are: kill the Jews and Americans, who are like them and who

249. *Süddeutsche Zeitung*, July 19, 2002.
250. Milton-Edwards, op. cit., pp. 113ff.

stand by them. They are all in one and the same trench fighting the Arabs and Muslims."[251]

"We are not in any way superstitious people" Hamas leader al-Zahar had told the *Süddeutsche Zeitung*'s readers. "We do not live with myths." Hamas' members, however, are "not superstitious" only insofar as they unconditionally believe in Allah. They live "without myths" only insofar as they believe in the literal truth of the Koran. Its members receive their high academic qualifications because for Hamas it is a sign of the greatest erudition to believe that Charles Darwin was a paid liar and Auschwitz a sanitary facility and that the Jews are the main enemy of humanity. In Islamist Newspeak, words such as "superstition," "myth" and "academic" mean the exact opposite of what secular societies understand them to mean.

Back to the Gaza strip of the year 1980. Outside the university, Islamist regimentation was being imposed by violence. In that year the office of the Palestinian Red Crescent (the Islamic equivalent of the Red Cross), which was run by a left-nationalist, was burned down along with its library. Throughout Gaza, cinemas, alcohol shops and restaurants serving alcohol were closed or demolished. Weddings that allegedly flouted Islamic tradition were attacked, and musical performances, western wedding dresses and association between the sexes prohibited at such celebrations. By 1987, according to Milton-Edwards, it had become well nigh impossible to find anyone not wearing conservative Islamic dress.[252]

But how did the Israeli occupying power react to the forces of *Mujama al-Islami*? In the hope of gaining a security advantage for itself, it gave free rein to the Islamist terror against the

---

251. Gal Ben-Ari, *Die Saat des Hasses, Juden und Israel in den arabischen Medien* (Holzgerlingen: Hänssler-Verlag, 2002), pp. 22 and 28. Halabiya was speaking in his capacity as a member of the PA-appointed "Fatwa Council."
252. It was not until 1990 that the PLO was able to break the Hamas monopoly in Gaza, with the foundation of a second university, the Al-Azhar, under its control. See Abu-Amr, op. cit., p. 254, note 14.

PLO and PFLP. The implications of the Islamists' ideology and methods were totally misread.

On the West Bank too Islamists, calling themselves Muslim Brothers, were the PLO's most important opponents.[253] Following the PLO's defeat in the Lebanon war in 1982 they were able to gain political ground. Their activities were, however, concentrated almost exclusively on the universities. Thus, as a result of fierce clashes between left-nationalists and Islamists, both Bir Zeit University and Najah University in Nablus were temporarily closed. Hebron University was spared such conflict purely and simply because the Islamists were clearly dominant there. The students there erected a special memorial to Afghan war veteran and Hamas founder Abdullah Azzam, who was especially revered as a shining example of the jihadi spirit.

So, first, Ahmed Yasin's movement had created a mass support base. Next, in the struggle against Palestinian opponents, they built up their organizational strongholds. Now they embarked on the third stage: confrontation with Israel. The trigger-point was the Palestinian popular uprising whose Arabic name, *intifada*, is best translated as "shaking-off" (of the Israeli occupiers).

The Hamas Charter

In December 1987 anger and frustration at the 20-year-long Israeli occupation of the Gaza strip and West Bank exploded in a spontaneous uprising sparked off by a road accident. Mass demonstrations in Gaza swiftly spread to the West Bank. All Israeli attempts to suppress the uprising only fanned the flames higher. When in January 1988 Hamas made its first public appearance, the struggle for hegemony within the Palestinian camp inten-

253. The West Bank (of the River Jordan), also known as "Judea and Samaria," which until its annexation by Israel in 1967 was under Jordanian control, has a population of some 2 million. 80% of the population are Muslim, 12% Jews and 8% Christians. The two largest towns are Nablus and Hebron, with 100,000 and 120,000 inhabitants respectively.

sified, with, on the one side, the nationalist "United National Leadership" supported by the PLO and, on the other, Hamas.[254] Now the Islamists cashed in on their network of social institutions. While at the beginning of the uprising the pro-PLO forces had the upper hand, by summer 1988 Hamas had already established temporary dominance: "For the first time in the Palestinian movement's history the Islamists had succeeded in imposing their will on the nationalists."[255]

The battle between the two lines first took the form of a paper war, with both sides issuing dozens of leaflets. Hamas' first leaflet from January 1988 opened with the following words: "Oh all our people, men and women. O our children: the Jews – brothers of the apes, assassins of the prophets, bloodsuckers, warmongers – are murdering you, depriving you of life after having plundered your homeland and your homes. Only Islam can break the Jews and destroy their dream." "Liberation," it goes on to proclaim, "will not be completed without sacrifice, blood and jihad that continues until victory." At the same time, all so-called collaborators were threatened with death. "Those who deal in betrayal have only themselves to blame. All of you are exposed and known."[256]

The last-mentioned point brings the second level of the intra-Palestinian conflict into focus. Following the pattern of the 1936-39 disturbances, during which the Mufti liquidated his Palestinian opponents, in the intifada 50 years later Palestinians were mainly killed by other Palestinians. "In the Israeli-occupied

254. The United National Leadership comprised Fatah, the People's Front for the Liberation of Palestine (PFLP), the Democratic Front for the Liberation of Palestine (DFLP) and the Communist Party. See Milton-Edwards op. cit., p. 145.
255. Kepel op. cit., p. 203. The second most important Islamist organization in Palestine, Islamic Jihad, is described by Yehudit Barsky in an article from July 2002 entitled "Islamic Jihad Movement in Palestine," which can be found at www.ajc.org .
256. Schaul Mishal and Reuben Aharoni, *Speaking Stones. Communiqués from the Intifada Underground* (Syracuse: Syracuse University Press, 1994), p. 201.

territories more Muslims were killed by [Hamas'] fundamentalist Qassam brigades than by the Israeli occupying troops."²⁵⁷ When in 1989 the Israeli government put 300 Hamas members on trial, they were charged with, among other things, "assassinating collaborators and brutally imposing the laws of the uprising on the population."²⁵⁸ The sort of methods used to impose these "laws of the uprising" on the population is made crystal clear in the study *Collaborators in the Occupied Territories* produced jointly by a Palestinian and an Israeli researcher. It reveals that at a cautious estimate at least 942 Palestinian men and women were murdered as "collaborators" between 1987 and 1993 alone. Among them were some 130 accused of "moral transgression" (drugs, "prostitution," "dealing in videos"). According to Milton-Edwards, "the execution of collaborators was viewed as a religious obligation and a means of protecting the religion in the face of Israel." However, there were also murders committed for purely personal motives.²⁵⁹

Thirdly, the Islamists exerted especially strong pressure on the PLO by adopting their own Charter. In every respect, Hamas' new document put the 1968 PLO Charter in the shade: while the PLO text seeks to justify the necessity for the elimination of Israel without recourse to overly blatant antisemitism, the Hamas Charter no longer exercises the slightest restraint in this regard. Here, the jihad against Israel is presented as the first step in a global anti-Jewish war of annihilation. The Hamas Charter probably ranks as one of contemporary Islamism's most important programmatic document and its significance goes far beyond the Palestine conflict.

257. Tibi 2000 op. cit., p. 24.
258. Milton-Edwards op. cit., p. 152.
259. Be'er, Yizhar and Saleh, Abdel-Jawad, "Collaborators in the Occupied Territories: Human Rights Abuses and Violations" (February 1995). This study can be found at http://www.btselem.org/Download/199401_Collaboration_Suspects_Eng.doc; Milton-Edwards op. cit., p. 157.

This document extols the Muslim Brotherhood as "the largest Islamic Movement in the modern era" and a "world organization." Hamas defines itself as the Palestinian branch of the Brotherhood and at the same time as a "universalistic movement," whose jihad should be supported by Muslims from all over the world. Accordingly, it is not just Israel, but "world Zionism" which is identified as the adversary. According to its Charter, Hamas regards itself as "the spearhead and the avant-garde" in the struggle against "world Zionism."[260]

This adversary has targeted Muslim women with quite exceptional malice. Thus, according to article 17 of the Charter: "The enemies have understood that role, therefore they realise that if they can guide and educate [the Muslim women] in a way that would distance them from Islam, they would have won that war." With these words, any stirring of freedom on the part of a Muslim woman is *a priori* condemned as direct or indirect collaboration with the enemy, a crime that is, of course, punishable by death. Hamas goes on to explain that the enemy exercises remote control of Muslim women through every conceivable means such as "publicity and movies, curricula of education and culture, using as their intermediaries their craftsmen who are part of the various Zionist Organizations which take on all sorts of names and shapes such as: the Freemasons, Rotary Clubs, gangs of spies and the like."

As the antidote to such dangers, the Charter advocates eradication, purges and prohibitions. "When Islam will retake possession of [the means to] guide the life [of the Muslims]," article 17 continues, "it will wipe out those organizations which are the enemy of humanity and Islam." Moreover, "there is no escape from introducing fundamental changes in educational curricula in order to cleanse them from all vestiges of the ideological invasion which has been brought about by orientalists

260. See articles 2, 7 and 32 of the Charter. An English translation can be found at www.palestinecenter.org/cpap/documents/charter.html.

and missionaries." The Charter even contains, in article 19, a ban on laughter: "All this is a serious matter, no jesting. For the *umma* fighting its jihad knows no jesting." Is not Islamism's whole essence contained in this single clause banning laughter?

As if the Charter's authors had had the pages of the *Protocols of the Elders of Zion* open before them as they drafted their text, "world Zionism" is held responsible for all the evils of world history. "The Jews stood behind the French and the communist Revolutions," "they stood behind World War I, so as to wipe out the Islamic Caliphate" and "they also stood behind World War II, where they collected immense benefits from trading with war materials." "They inspired the establishment of the United Nations and the Security Council ... in order to rule the world by their intermediary. There was no war that broke out anywhere without their fingerprints on it." In their struggle for world domination, the annexation of Palestine is a step on the way to expansion "from the Nile to the Euphrates." Then, "they will look forward to more expansion etc." And here, finally, in article 32, the source is named: "Their scheme has been laid out in the *Protocols of the Elders of Zion*, and their present [conduct] is the best proof of what is said there."

One might be inclined simply to shrug one's shoulders at such madness, in the same way as Adolf Hitler's ravings were once met with a pitying smile. But it is precisely this delusion that inspires the Palestinian enthusiasm for the suicidal mass murder of Israeli civilians and provides the phantasmagorical motive for Hamas' goal of destroying Israel. Through its Charter, Hamas follows faithfully in the footsteps of Amin el-Husseini, the Mufti of Jerusalem.

Amazingly, this most obvious of explanatory sources, Hamas' program, very rarely gets a mention in the interminable journalistic musings about the motivation for suicide bombing. This gives new relevance to the warning issued by Léon Poliakov in 1969 that "anyone who does not denounce antisemitism in its primitive and elementary form, and does not do so precisely because it is primitive and elementary, will have to face the question as to whether he is not thereby sending out a sign of secret approval to anti-Semites all over the world."[261]

Hamas' conclusions on the fate of Israel are in any case unambiguously spelt out in the Charter. According to article 6, Hamas will "raise the banner of Allah over every inch of Palestine…. There is no solution to the Palestinian problem except by jihad. The initiatives, proposals and International Conferences are but a waste of time, an exercise in futility." The Charter's view of the PLO, on the other hand, is remarkably benevolent. "Can a Muslim turn away from his father, his brother, his relative or his friend?" asks the Charter in reference to the PLO. "When the PLO adopts Islam as the guideline for life, then we shall become its soldiers." But why this moderate tone? Where does the hope that the PLO too will sooner or later pursue "the path of Islam" as Hamas understands it, stem from?

El-Husseini and Arafat

The still current image of the PLO was established in 1974 as the Vietnam War was drawing to a close. In the very same year Yasser Arafat stood with a gun in his belt before the United Nations General Assembly able to bask in his role as the new symbol of worldwide anti-imperialism. Promoted by the Soviet Union's propaganda machine, the Arab League, the Organization of Islamic Countries and the Non-Aligned Movement, the PLO's *fedayeen* (the self-sacrificing ones) began to take over the place in the anti-imperialist worldview previously occupied by the Vietcong.

Even at the time an examination of the PLO's 1968 Charter would have revealed that organization's non-progressive nature,

261. Léon Poliakov, *Vom Antizionismus zum Antisemitismus* (Freiburg: ca ira, 1992), p. 104.

apparent for instance from its adherence to the *völkisch* principle.

The biggest problem, and one that had already preoccupied the Mufti of Jerusalem, was the concern that the Palestinian refugees might be accepted into citizenship and thus treated like citizens by the Arab host states. In writings, speeches and conference interventions, Amin el-Husseini fought tirelessly to prevent this.[262] This same concern was later addressed in articles 4 and 5 of the PLO Charter through a rigid *jus sanguinis* rule: "The Palestinian identity is a genuine, essential, and inherent characteristic; it is transmitted from parents to children." "Anyone born, after that date [1947], of a Palestinian father – whether inside Palestine or outside it – is also a Palestinian,"[263] This definition, which attempted to perpetuate the existence of refugee camps in Arab countries as a means of pressure against Israel, was based on the *völkisch* principle and had nothing whatsoever to do with anything progressive. No less reactionary is the goal stated in article 15, that the PLO "aims at the elimination of Zionism in Palestine" - i.e. the destruction of Israel - and the claim that the 1947 United Nations' partition plan and the creation of the State of Israel were "entirely illegal." The notion of the Jewish world conspiracy surfaces in the statement in article 22 that "Israel is a constant source of threat vis-à-vis peace in the Middle East and the whole world" and the characterization of Zionism as "a political movement organically associated with international imperialism." Finally, the idea of jihad too appears in secular guise. Every Palestinian, we read in article 7, "must be prepared for the armed struggle and ready to sacrifice his wealth and his life in order to win back his homeland.... Armed struggle is the only way to liberate Pal-

---

262. Zvi Elpeleg, *The Grand Mufti. Hajj Amin al-Hussaini, Founder of the Palestinian National Movement* (London: Frank Cass, 1993), pp. 136ff.
263. The PLO Charter is reproduced in Laqueur/Rubin, op. cit., pp.366-372.

estine." The Charter does not wastes a single word on the social or political nature of this "liberation."

The actual role of Islamism in the political evolution of PLO Chairman Yasser Arafat remains hidden by this phraseology. Post-1987, with the incipient Islamization of Palestinian politics, this aspect gained in importance – grounds for taking a closer look at Arafat's intellectual development.

Yasser Arafat, whose full name, Rahman Abdul Rauf Arafat el-Kudwa el-Husseini, reveals him to be a distant relative of the Mufti of Jerusalem, was born in 1929. He spent his childhood in Jerusalem, where he had no greater hero than the Mufti. At the age of seven he had already participated in the Mufti-inspired revolt by throwing stones.[264]

From 1942 onwards Arafat spent his youth in Cairo, where he frequented pro-German Egyptian circles. In 1946 the Mufti was allowed to return to Cairo and Arafat often spent time with him there. Abdel Kader el-Husseini, a relative of the Mufti and a leader of anti-Zionist armed gangs in Palestine, returned from time to time to Cairo to organise young volunteers. "'He was my leader. I was seventeen and ... one of the youngest officers,' recalled Arafat. In Abdel Kader's kitchen, young Palestinians learned to make bombs and defuse them; on different occasions Arafat and other students were secretly trained to be commandos by a German officer who had travelled with Hajj Amin [el-Husseini] to Egypt."[265] For two years during this period Arafat is said to have organized weapons supplies to el-Husseini's secret organization for use against Israel. Together with a group of Muslim Brothers, which he had joined, Arafat set off for the war against the founding of Israel. In 1950 he again left his engineering college in order to conduct attacks with Muslim Brothers on British troops in

264. The following account draws heavily on the biography written in 1992 by Janet Wallach and John Wallach, op. cit. and that written in 1990 by Andrew Gowers and Tony Walker, *Arafat, Hinter dem Mythos* (Hamburg: Europäische Verlagsanstalt, 1994).
265. Wallach/Wallach, op. cit., p. 71.

the Canal Zone. Finally in 1952 - encouraged by el-Husseini and backed by the Brotherhood - he was elected Chairman of the Palestinian Student Association. Arafat was also initially on the best of terms with Nasser and the Free Officers. However, following the 1954 assassination attempt he was imprisoned as a known supporter of the Muslim Brotherhood.

Like many other Muslim Brothers of the Nasser period, in 1957 Yasser Arafat went to Saudi Arabia, where in 1959, together with Khalil al-Wazir, later to become famous under the *nom de guerre* Abu Jihad (Father of the Jihad), he founded Fatah. Their first project was a newspaper, *Our Palestine*, which advocated renewed military attacks on Israel. At this time, Fatah's activities were financed primarily from the coffers of the Mufti, Amin el-Husseini, whose patronage of Fatah was, however, more than just material in nature. As late as 1967 and 1968, one of the Mufti's son-in-laws, Muheideen el-Husseini, reported, Arafat and el-Husseini used to meet at his house in Amman. "Hajj Amin [el-Husseini] felt that Arafat would be the right leader for the Palestinian nation after him. He thought he could bear the responsibility."[266]

The propaganda successes of Fatah, which Nasser considered a front organization for the Muslim Brothers, led the Egyptian leader to found the PLO as an intended counterweight - a step which el-Husseini, considering this PLO far too moderate, strongly opposed. "Both Hajj Amin and Fatah were of the opinion that terrorist activity beyond the armistice lines with Israel should be encouraged, in order to elicit reprisal action and thus push the Arab states into an all-out war against Israel."[267] Saudi Arabia too backed Fatah at this juncture, since its cooperation with the anti-Nasser Muslim Brothers fitted in with Saudi policy at that time.[268]

266. Cited in Wallach/Wallach, op. cit., p. 280.
267. Elpeleg, op. cit., 147.
268. Gowers and Walker, op. cit., p. 58.

The Six-Day War of 1967 marked a turning point in this dispute. Fatah continued to strike the same rhetorical note as before. "[We washed] away the shame of defeat [the 1967 war] with the blood of our martyrs," they declared in 1968. "We openly declared the jihad among the ranks of our youth and we gave up the best of them on that path."[269] The PLO, however, was totally transformed, with Fatah now joining the PLO and becoming the dominant force within it, a situation that persists to this day. A few months later Yasser Arafat was named as the new PLO Chairman. At the instigation of el-Husseini, who introduced Arafat to the Saudi King Faisal, Saudi money too now began to flow to the PLO.[270]

It is this prehistory that explains why the Hamas Charter takes such a positive attitude to the PLO. While the PLO's various changes of direction may have depended not on the Koran, but on its financial backers or the spirit of the times, Arafat and Yassin were always of one and the same mind on the most important political and religious issues.

Firstly, Arafat never lost sight of the goal of the obliteration of Israel. "Peace for us means the destruction of Israel," he declared to the Venezuelan daily *El Mundo* in 1980. "We are preparing for an all-out war, a war which will last for generations."[271] For him, the agreement signed in Oslo in 1993 on the creation of a Palestinian Autonomous Area was only a temporary tactical manoeuvre, as Arafat intimated by a reference to Islamic history: "We respect agreements the way that the Prophet Muhammad and Salah al-Din [SaLadin] respected the agreements which they signed."[272] The truces in question were of course signed in periods of weakness and were broken by the Islamic leaders as soon as they were strong enough.

269. Nels Johnson, op. cit., p. 75.
270. Wallach/Wallach, op. cit., p. 335.
271. Cited in Wistrich, op. cit., p. 185.
272. Yossef Bodansky, *Bin Laden. The Man Who Declared War on America* (Rocklin: Prima Publishing, 1999), p. 278.

The refusal to recognise Israel is manifested in particular in the fact that all the Palestinian Authority's (PA) new post-Oslo schoolbooks and maps make no mention of Israel or Jewish history. Even the most up-to-date maps used in PA schools anticipate the destruction of Israel: between Jordan and the Mediterranean only a unified Arab Palestine can be seen.[273]

Secondly, for Yassin and Arafat the subject of the Holocaust - the central experience in the establishment and attitudes of the State of Israel – has remained taboo, as has that of the role of the Mufti in National Socialism. No post-Oslo PA schoolbook so much as mentions Auschwitz. When a PA official asked that this be changed, he was met with furious protests and the request was rejected. The Chairman of the Palestinian Parliament's Education Committee declared that, "we have no interest in teaching the Holocaust." His parliamentary colleague and Fatah leader, Hatem Abd al-Qader, added that teaching about the Holocaust would present "a great danger" for the Palestinian identity. "If such a decision [about teaching the Holocaust] is made, it will undoubtedly ruin the Palestinian dream and aspirations. It will entirely obliterate the past, present and future of the Palestinians."[274] Not the slightest danger to the Palestinian identity, though, seemed to be presented by the circulation with express PA approval of Hitler's programmatic work *Mein Kampf*, which reached number six in the Palestinian Territory's bestsellers' list in 1999. The translator of the Arabic edition refers in his introduction to his author's continued relevance: "Adolf Hitler does not belong to the German people alone, he is one of the few great men who almost stopped the motion of history, altered its course..... National Socialism did not die with the

273. Götz Nordbruch, *Narrating Palestinian Nationalism. A Study of the New Palestinian Textbooks* (Washington, The Middle East Media Research Institute, 2002), pp. 14 and 22.
274. "Palestinians Debate Including the Holocaust in the Curriculum," *MEMRI Special Dispatch* no. 187, February 21, 2001.

death of its herald. Rather, its seeds multiplied under each star."[275] While the PA "sows" the seeds of National Socialism in this way, and reaps a harvest of murderous anti-Jewish actions from it, Israeli policy is presented in all its media as a continuation or even intensification of Nazism. The constant equation of Israeli and National Socialist policies - "Nazism of the Jews," "Nazi-like enemy," "Nazi-Zionist practices" - amounts to a specific form of Holocaust denial, one which legitimates the pursuit of an anti-Jewish extermination policy, while projecting these murderous intentions onto the chosen victim.

Thirdly, as a pious Muslim, Arafat remained to the end of his days committed to jihad. On a pilgrimage to Mecca in 1978 he gave a remarkable speech in which he defined the struggle for the "liberation" of Jerusalem as an obligation of every Muslim. "I declare from here" he proclaimed, "from the land of the Prophet, from the cradle of Islam, the opening of the gate of holy war for the liberation of Palestine and the recovery of Jerusalem."[276] In the course of the Al-Aqsa intifada Arafat stepped up his religious rhetoric. Along with his repeatedly expressed wish to die a "martyr's" death, he described Palestine in a television address as the "territory of the *ribat*," using a religious term denoting the front line in the jihad against the unbelievers.[277] Is it any wonder that in the post-Oslo books for sixth and seventh grade pupils jihad and martyrdom are extolled in terms such as these: "the noble soul has two goals: death and the desire for it," and that the war for every square meter of Islamic land is declared a religious duty?[278]

"When the PLO adopts Islam as the guideline for life, then we shall become its soldiers" Hamas stated in its 1988 Charter. Ten years later, the PLO would fall in behind the Islamists.

275. "Hitlers Mein Kampf in East Jerusalem and PA Territories," *MEMRI Special Dispatch* no. 48, October 1, 1999.
276. Johnson, op. cit., p. 75.
277. Joseph Croitoru, "Was ist Ribat?," *FAZ*, December 18, 2001.
278. Nordbruch 2002, op. cit., p. 17.

Mass Murder as Strategy

Between the first intifada of 1987 and the second, which began in autumn 2000, lies a profound gulf. The first uprising took place within the context of the Cold War. In mid-1988 references were still being made in the communiqués of the PLO-controlled United National Leadership to Soviet friendship.[279] Despite the loss of momentum, the existence of the Soviet bloc still provided an underpinning for the PLO's secularism. The intifada consequently ended in traditional style; peace talks under superpower auspices in Madrid, then a treaty between the PLO and Israel following secret talks in Oslo. The second intifada, however, began in a totally different context.

Since 1990 Islamism has been constantly advancing in Palestine for a number of reasons. Firstly, with the disappearance from the scene of the socialist countries that had supported them, the ground vanished from beneath the feet of the secular anti-imperialist elements in the PLO. The ideological vacuum was filled by Islamism. "After the fall of Marxism, Islam replaced it," declared Ahmad Khomeini, the son of the Iranian Ayatollah in 1991.[280] And indeed, since then, Islamism has been the only remaining force which presents a consistent ideological alternative to capitalism, is endowed with enormous financial resources and has global reach.

Secondly, in 1993 Hamas adopted the tactic of suicidal mass murder, thereby outbidding the PLO on the field of action. The first suicide bombing took place on April 16, 1993.[281]

Later in February 1994, Baruch Goldstein, a radical right-wing Jewish settler, shot 29 Muslims at prayer in a mosque in Hebron. The second successful suicide attack of Hamas followed on April 13, 1994. While the Hebron massacre inspired horror and immediate political counter-measures in Israel, the response

279. Mishal and Aharoni, op. cit., p. 84.
280. Bodansky, op. cit., p. XVI.
281. Joseph Croitoru, *Hamas* (München: Beck Verlag, 2007), p. 128.

to the Hamas massacres in the Palestinian Autonomous Territory was the opposite. Hamas was able unchallenged to put out video recordings of the heroic testaments of its mass murderers for publicity and propaganda purposes.[282]

After July 1994 Arafat's officials had sole police powers in the Territories. By proceeding undeterred to further massacres, Hamas also put twofold pressure on the PLO. The PLO's initial efforts to prevent such murders were condemned as collaboration with Israel. When in November 1994 the newly established Palestinian police force opened fire on a Hamas demonstration killing 16 people, Arafat's popularity hit rock bottom.[283] At the same time, the suicide massacres served the strategic goal of helping to bring the most anti-PLO parties to power in Israel. Thus, carefully calibrated attacks led to the election first of Binyamin Netanyahu in 1996 and then of Ariel Sharon four years later.

In 2000, suicide murder became the defining feature of the second intifada. It was a coolly calculated instrument of policy whose tactical rationale is set out in the Hamas Charter: to blow to smithereens even the most tentative attempts at Israeli-Arab dialogue. But above and beyond their tactical purpose, the anti-Jewish massacres have a programmatic significance. The *way* in which Jews are killed indicates *why* they are being killed. The targets of the attacks are not senior politicians or military personnel, but crowds of civilians, regardless of whether they are religious or secular, young or old, supporters or opponents of Sharon. The more innocent people are killed, mutilated and injured, the greater the attack's success. The sharper the edges of the metal splinters and nails in the bomb, the more valuable it is. Anyone who kills in this way is translating a specific Islamist-fascist worldview into action. This worldview's antisemitism, in which the Jews are demonized as absolute evil, inevitably produces the intention of destroying this evil across the globe.

282. Milton-Edwards, op. cit., pp. 166ff.
283. Kepel, op. cit., pp. 388ff.

The new suicidal mass murder strategy has been vigorously supported by other prominent Muslim Brothers. One who has particularly distinguished himself in this respect is a man who has made a reputation throughout the Arab world as a television preacher, a Muslim Brother from Egypt, Sheikh Yusuf Qaradawi, who has lived in Qatar since 1961 from where, since 1996, he has been broadcasting his weekly program "Life and Islamic Law" to the Arab masses on *al-Jazeera*. While Islam prohibits suicide, Qaradawi explicitly supported Hamas' practice in his *fatwa* entitled, "Hamas Operations Are Jihad and Those Who [Carry it Out and] Are Killed are Considered Martyrs." ... "In December 2001 Al-Qaradawi elaborated on his stance regarding suicide bombings by articulating the position that there are no innocent Israeli civilians: 'In Israel, all men and women are soldiers. They are all occupying troops.'"[284]

In addition, Ahmed Yassin was able to notch up foreign policy successes. In 1998 he embarked on a triumphant tour of the Arab world calling for the liquidation of the Oslo Agreement and Israel, in the course of which he had a lucrative audience with the Saudi king. Yassin returned to the Gaza strip weighed down with 25 million dollars from the Saudi treasury alone.[285]

Both unwilling and incapable of conducting a principled struggle with Islamism, the PLO sank ever deeper into the Islamist mire. Following Israel's voluntary withdrawal of its troops from southern Lebanon in May 2000 (although the Islamists insisted that the "Zionist army" had been driven out by Hizbollah), Arafat swept aside the offer made at Camp David of Palestinian control of 96% of the West Bank, incited a new intifada in September 2000 and released 120 Hamas terrorists

284. Rainer Hermann, "Fernsehprediger," *FAZ*, November 10, 2001 and Yehudit Barsky, "Hamas – the Islamic Resistance Movement of Palestine," February 2002, p. 3. This can be found at www.ajc.org .
285. Bodansky, op. cit., pp. 276ff; *MEMRI Special Dispatch* no. 3, July 30, 1998; Barsky on Hamas, op. cit., p. 4.

from his jails as the opening shot in the new uprising.[286] Unlike the 1987 intifada, however, this time Hamas had the initiative from the start. Its suicide bombing strategy was copied by all the "secular" Palestinian groups and the line between a movement of "liberation" and one of extermination was systematically blurred. "After the fall of Marxism, Islam replaced it" Khomeini's son had prophesied in 1991 and, he continued, "as long as Islam exists, U.S. hostility exists, and as long as U.S. hostility exists, the struggle exists." He warned against restricting the struggle to the Middle East alone, "because the struggle against Israel is a war against the U.S. and Europe with no short end."[287] The struggle against Israel as war against the USA; it is scarcely possible better to capture the message of September 11. What was the impact of this attack on Islamism in Palestine and the wider Arab world?

286. The remarkable success of the uprising launched by the *völkisch*-Muslim UCK (Kosovo Liberation Army) in summer 1998 in Kosovo may perhaps have contributed to the decision to launch a new intifada. In a statement issued in London in summer 1999, Islamist organizations drew a clear parallel between the situation in Kosovo and that in Palestine, declaring that " we shall not end the jihad against the Serb or Israeli occupiers, whatever the UN may say or do." Previously, the UCK, against Serbia and with respect to the NATO states, had successfully done what Fatah had long tried to do, i.e. to provoke Israeli "revenge actions" by carrying out acts of terrorism and so push the Arab states into an all-out war with Israel. According to a report issued by the NATO Parliamentary Assembly in December 2000, "UCK attacks" were deliberately designed to escalate the conflict "in order to create a humanitarian crisis, which would move NATO to take action." See Dieter S. Lutz, "Krieg nach Gefühl," *FAZ*, December 15, 2000. Many interesting parallels can be drawn between the UCK and the PLO/ Hamas. In both cases, terror was and is used against "collaborators'; both movements, pursuing a strategy of tension, brought death and misery on their own people and deliberately exacerbated humanitarian problems (for example, Kosovo Albanians were forced to remain in refugee camps) in order to stoke up the crisis with the help of professional PR strategists. See M. Küntzel, *Der Weg in den Krieg. Deutschland, die NATO und das Kosovo* (Berlin: Elefanten Press, 2000), pp. 114ff and 178.
287. Bodansky, op. cit., p. XVI.

Chapter Four

· · · · · · · · · · · · · · · ·

September 11 and Israel

Forcing hundreds of airplane passengers to take part in one's own suicide in order to immolate thousands at their workplaces is monstrous and outrageous. But Clausewitz's famous dictum remains valid for this form of warfare too: 9/11 was the prosecution of politics by other means.

Osama bin Laden has repeatedly explained the purpose of this policy. Unlike Qutb, who called for priority to be given to the struggle against apostate Muslims, bin Laden considers the USA and Israel to be enemy number one. Of course, he also wants to bring about the fall of all the "unbelieving" regimes in the Arab world. But he sees this as impossible as long as the Americans have not been driven from the Arabian Peninsula and the Jews from Palestine.

"Bin Laden argued the Islamic Jihad, like all other Islamist terrorist organizations, must 'turn its guns' on Israel and the United States instead of Egypt, Saudi Arabia, or the other Arab countries," was how Albanian jihadist Ahmad Ibrahim al-Najjar reported a discussion with Bin Laden at the beginning of 1998. "Without the eviction of the United States from the Middle East and the destruction of Israel, it would be virtually impossible for the Islamist forces to defeat the 'puppet regimes' bolstered by the United States."[288]

Despite the craziness as regards to goals, a comprehensive strategy is discernible here and suicide attacks such as that of 11 September are part and parcel of it. In March 2001, bin Laden's

288. Cited in Bodansky, op. cit., p. 222ff.

deputy, Ayman al-Zawahiri, set out the rationale for 9/11 in his book *Knights under the Prophet's Banner*: "[Terror attacks] bring the greatest possible horror on the enemy with relatively small losses for the Islamist movement." The best attacks are those that kill the most civilians since "this spreads maximum terror among the peoples of the West. This is a language they understand."[289]

Many Western observers, however, prefer to ignore the political purpose of 9/11, stubbornly holding on to the view that the murder of American civilians by bin Laden and that of Israeli civilians by Hamas are two totally different things.

In Europe, this "ignorance" about the antisemitic background of 9/11 offers political advantages. It furthers European resentment of the USA and enables the advocates of anti-Americanism to present even the killing of 3,000 civilians as an act of resistance. Karl Lamers, foreign policy spokesman until 2002 for the conservative CDU/CSU group in the German Parliament, expressed the sentiments of countless anti-globalists and anti-imperialists when he declared in an interview with the *taz* newspaper, which is close to the German Green Party, "I claim that September 11 is only the most radical expression of the revolt against western dominance, embodied above all by the USA."[290] As the following pages will demonstrate, however, the attack on the World Trade Centre was inseparable from the aim of obliterating Israel. To prove our case, we shall refer first to the history of the Muslim Brothers, since it turns out that al-Qa'ida is closely connected to the Brotherhood and its successor organizations in both programmatic and personal terms.

Bin Laden and the Muslim Brothers

1979 was a crucial year in the annals of Islamism from two points of view. Just as in their day the French and Russian revolutions

---

289. Cited in Julia Gerlach, "Bin Ladens Schriftsteller," *Berliner Zeitung*, March 8, 2002.
290. Interview with Karl Lamers, *taz*, July 9, 2002.

were hailed as bringers of hope, so did the Islamists greet Khomeini's victory in Iran as a triumph for their approach. Hard on the heels of this euphoria came a shock, as in the very same year, the Red Army took control of Muslim Afghanistan, creating a new focus for the holy war. Among the first Arabs to organize jihad against the Soviet Union was the man who probably exerted the strongest influence on bin Laden, the Muslim Brother Abdallah Azzam.

Azzam, born in 1941 in Jenin, today under Palestinian control, embodied to a greater extent than anyone else, the links between the Palestinian and Afghan fronts of the Islamist jihad. "Azzam was one of the founders of the Palestinian-Islamist terrorist organization Hamas" recounts Khalid Duran in the magazine *TransIslam.* "All his life he had to defend himself against the reproach that his Afghanistan intervention was a distraction from Palestine, which was in the last analysis the 'central concern for Islam'. In fact, Azzam wished seriously to fight for Afghanistan, in order there to create the basis for the subsequent struggle against Israel."[291]

In 1960 Azzam was appointed the Muslim Brotherhood's spokesman at Damascus University. Between 1971 and 1973 he studied for his PhD at Egypt's al-Azhar University, where he made contact with militant Egyptian Islamists. He then went on teach compulsory courses in Islam at the King Abd al-Aziz University in Jeddah in Saudi Arabia, a city in which the influence of the Egyptian Muslim Brothers was especially strong. Not only was it the entry point for printed material from Egypt, but Muhammad Qutb, brother of Sayyid Qutb, who had been hanged in Egypt in 1966, also taught courses in compulsory Islam at the University and distributed his brother's writings there.

Osama bin Laden, who studied as a disciple of Muhammad Qutb in Jeddah, familiarized himself with Sayyid Qutb's writings

291. Khalid Duran, "Der einen Teufel, der anderen Held," *FAZ*, September 20, 2001.

between 1974 and 1978. Qutb's texts would become part of the training program at all the training camps that bin Laden later established in Afghanistan.[292] However, the strongest personal relationship bin Laden developed was with his other university teacher, the Palestinian Azzam, whose lectures unfailingly revolved around one central topic: jihad instead of negotiations with Israel, jihad instead of conferences about Afghanistan, jihad instead of dialogue with the unbelievers. With unrivalled fervor Azzam propagated the martyrdom cult. Throughout his writings, he extolled the achievement of sainthood or, more precisely, heavenly self-ennoblement through jihadist self-destruction as the proper aim in life of every pious Muslim.[293]

In 1982, with his pupil Osama bin Laden, Azzam founded the Mujahideen Services Bureau in the Pakistani city of Peshawar and launched the magazine al-Jihad. In all his writings, he never forgot to emphasise that the struggle in Palestine was just as much a duty for every Muslim as the one in Afghanistan.[294] In addition, in 1984 bin Laden set up the House of the Companions of the Prophet as a staging post for the "Arab Afghans." As the holder of a degree in public administration, he established a database of all the jihadists who passed through. Soon this coordination centre would become known simply as al-Qa'ida (the Base).

In the same year as the founding of the House of the Companions, another confidant of bin Laden, Ayman al-Zawahiri, was released from prison in Egypt. Zawahiri embodied like no one else the stages in Islamism's radicalization process. Born in 1951, he joined the Muslim Brothers when still young. In 1974 he completed his studies in Cairo as a paediatrician. In the 1970s

292. Kepel, op. cit., p. 374; Bassam Tibi, "Ein mit Haß erfülltes Bild des Westens," Weltwoche, October 18, 2001.
293. Bodansky, op. cit., p. 11; Khalid Duran, "Lieblicher Geruch. Selbstmordattentäter und Märtyrerkult," FAZ, September 24, 2001.
294. Bodansky, op. cit., p. 11; Kepel, op. cit., pp. 181 and 374; Bassam Tibi, op. cit., Weltwoche, October 18, 2001.

he abandoned his doctor's practice in order to devote himself to the armed struggle to establish an Islamic dictatorship. At the start of the 1980s he was involved in the preparations for the assassination of Sadat. Jailed in 1981, he was released as early as 1984. In 1985 he joined the Mujahideen (warriors of jihad) in Afghanistan, where in 1995 he became bin Laden's deputy.[295]

It was under Zawahiri's influence that bin Laden adopted the view that the armed and terrorist struggle should take priority over teaching and propaganda.[296] Moreover, it was Al-Zawahiri too who convinced bin Laden of the need for the above-mentioned reorientation of jihadist strategy according to which, while jihad should continue to be waged against unbelieving governments in the Arab countries, the Americans and Israelis should now be the primary targets.

As a professional revolutionary, Zawahiri always paid particular attention to the indoctrination of his troops. This is demonstrated by information on his recruiting practices revealed during trials in Egypt. Practical training in bomb making, passport forgery, etc. was always preceded by intensive theoretical courses on topics such as "Islamic law," "ideology of Islamic jihad" and "the political history of militant Islamic movements."[297] In this way the link was maintained between each new generation of fighters and the origins of the Muslim Brothers. Osama bin Laden too is a product of that ideology and that history. The Egyptian influence on his actions is illustrated by the October 2001 video with which he responded to the US attacks on the Taliban: it shows bin Laden between two Egyptian jihadist leaders. On his left is the Egyptian Muhammad Atef, at the time al-Qa'ida's military chief, and on his right is Ayman al-Zawahiri, who, speaking after bin Laden, makes a veritable programmatic

295. Rainer Hermann, "Stellvertreter und Anwärter auf die Nachfolger Bin Ladens" *FAZ*, October 1, 2001.
296. Kepel, op. cit., 498; Bodansky, op. cit., p. 309.
297. Susan Sachs, "An Investigation in Egypt Illustrates Al-Qaeda's Web," *NYT*, November 21, 2001.

statement: "America is supreme among criminals, because it created this Israel, this fifty-year-long crime."[298]

Hatred of America

Al-Qa'ida's view of the USA is made up of a welter of overlapping antisemitic fantasies. The first and crudest is the distorted image of New York as a Jewish metropolis in which, therefore, virtually every bomb hits the right target.

This idea had already played a role in the 1993 attack on the World Trade Centre. The man behind this was Ramzi Ahmed Yousef, later jailed in the USA, who between 1992 and 1995 had lived in Azzam and bin Laden's Mujahideen Centre in Peshawar. In 1995 Yousef stated in an interview that, "he had chosen the World Trade Centre as a target because he wanted to make one tower fall into the other and so kill 250,000 people in total."[299]

Abdul Rahman Yasin, who took part in the planning of the 1993 attack, provided further details on its prehistory: "I want to blow up the Jewish neighbourhood of Brooklyn," Ramzi Yousef had told him at the beginning. After reconnoitring the New York neighbourhoods of Crown Heights and Williamsburg, however, Yousef amended this plan. "Instead, let's make one big bang, rather than several small ones in the Jewish neighbourhoods," he proposed, referring to the World Trade Centre. "Most of the people working in the World Trade Centre are Jews."[300]

The same lunatic idea motivated the perpetrators of 9/11. The first trial of a core member of the Hamburg al-Qa'ida cell, which took place between October 2002 and February 2003 in

298. Cited in John F. Burns, "Bin Laden Taunts US and Praises Hijackers," *NYT*, October 8, 2001.
299. Judith Miller, Dan von Natta Jr., "US Long Underestimated Al-Qaeda's Scope, Officials Say," *NYT*, June 9, 2002
300. CBS News' hour-long interview with Abdul Rahman Yasin is reported by Tina Kelley, "Suspect in 1993 Bombing Says Trade Center Wasn't First Target," NYT, June 1, 2002. For the background to this attack see Laurie Mylroie, *Study of Revenge* (Washington DC: The AEI Press, 2000). Christian Eggers, op. cit., p. XX: see also: *Der Spigel*, no. 36/2002, p. 117.

Hamburg, provided remarkable insight into the perpetrators' minds, despite being widely ignored by the German and international media.

The accused, Mounir el-Motassadeq, had been a close friend of Mohammed Atta, the ringleader of the 9/11 hijackers. One witness, Shahid Nickels, a member of Mohammed Atta's core group between 1998 and 2000, said the following: "Atta's *Weltanschauung* was based on a National Socialist way of thinking. He was convinced that 'the Jews' are determined to achieve world domination. He considered New York City to be the centre of world Jewry which was, in his opinion, Enemy Number One."

This trial in Hamburg also brought to light the second delusion underlying the Islamist view of America: that Jews control all the levers of American power. Thus, Shahid Nickels testified about the assailants' core group that: "They were convinced that Jews control the American government as well as the media and the economy of the United States. ... Motassadeq shared Atta's attitude in believing that a worldwide conspiracy of Jews exists. According to him, Americans want to dominate the world so that Jews can pile up capital."[301]

This is, in fact, al-Qa'ida's official position, expressed on many occasions by bin Laden himself. This is apparent, for example, from a closer look at his *Letter to the American People* of October 2002, where he explains why he considers the United States to be "the worst civilization witnessed by the history of mankind." His first reason is that, "You are the nation who, rather than ruling by the Sharia of Allah in its Constitution and Laws, choose to invent your own laws as you will and desire." Here we have the very essence of the Islamist program: away with democratic self-determination! Obey Allah and his holy law!

"The first thing," he continues, "that we are calling you to is Islam.... We call you... to reject the immoral acts of fornication,

---

301. Christian Eggers, op. cit.. See also *Der Spiegel*, no. 36/2002, p. 117.

homosexuality, intoxicants, gambling, and trading with interest."

However, for his second reason why the Americans are "the worst civilization," bin Laden focuses on the group he believes to be responsible for all the above-mentioned machinations. "In all its different forms and guises, the Jews have taken control of your economy, through which they have taken control of your media, and now control all aspects of your life making you their servants and achieving their aims at your expense; ... your law is the law of the rich and wealthy people.... Behind them stand the Jews, who control your policies, media and economy." [302]

This antisemitism has nothing to do with the policies of the Bush administration, as is clear from bin Laden's "Frontline interview" of May 1998 where he declares with reference to the Clinton administration that, "We believe that this administration represents Israel inside America. Take the sensitive ministries such as the Ministry of Exterior and the Ministry of Defence and the CIA, you will find that the Jews have the upper hand in them. They make use of America to further their plans for the world, especially the Islamic world. American presence in the Gulf provides support to the Jews and protects their rear." He later continued: "The enmity between us and the Jews goes far back in time and is deep rooted. There is no question that war between the two of us is inevitable." [303]

It is astonishing that this undisguised antisemitism has to date received so little attention in discussions about the motives for 9/11. Even the official 9/11 report from the American National Commission on Terrorist Attacks Upon the United States of July 2004 has a special blind spot in this respect, mentioning antisemitism only in relation to Mohammad Atta's Hamburg al-

302. Bin Laden's "Letter" is reproduced in full in: Observer Worldview, November 24, 2002 (see: http://observer.guardian.co.uk/worldview/story/0,11581,845725,00.html).
303. See: www.ontology.buffalo.edu/smith/courses01/rrtw/Laden.htm

Qa'ida cell. In the analysis of al-Qa'ida's ideology, on the other hand, it is not referred to at all. In the chapter entitled "Bin Laden's worldview," the report notes, accurately enough, that "Bin Laden relies heavily on the Egyptian writer Sayyid Qutb" and quotes from the above-mentioned *Letter to the American People.* Yet there is no mention of either Sayyid Qutb's antisemitism or the antisemitic content of the *Letter.*[304]

The third facet of jihadist anti-Americanism is based on a mind-set also found among anti-globalization activists: the obsessive division of the world between victimhood and guilt. Mythologizing themselves as permanent victims and refusing to accept any responsibility for their own fate, the USA is held responsible for any and every ill besetting Muslims. According to Suleiman Abu Gheith, an al-Qa'ida spokesman: "America is the reason for all the oppression, injustice, licentiousness, or suppression that is the Muslims' lot. It stands behind all the disasters that were caused and are still being caused to the Muslims."[305] Substitute "people" for "Muslims" in Abu Gheith's philippic and what would anti-globalization activists find to disagree with here?

Even when bin Laden's "World Islamic Front for Jihad against the Jews and Crusaders" denounces the exploitation of the Arabian Peninsula by American oil firms and the stationing of US troops in Saudi Arabia, this form of anti-imperialism has about as much to do with even the most elementary emancipatory critique of imperialism as do the anti-American tirades of Khomeini's successors: absolutely nothing. The aim of the Islamists' religious war is neither individual freedom nor the self-determination of dependent states, but the establishment of a total regime based purely and simply on submission to Allah and his

304. See "The 9/11 Commission Report," pp. 50-52.
305. 'Why We Fight America': Al-Qa'ida Spokesman Explains September 11 and Declares Intentions to Kill 4 Million Americans with Weapons of Mass Destruction, MEMRI Special Dispatch, June 18, 2002, p. 2.

deputies, the Caliphs. Their struggle is merely aimed against those aspects of imperialism and modernity that threaten the foundations of their despotic and patriarchal rule.

The fourth facet of al-Qaʻida's critique of the USA focuses on American support for Israel. This point was already made in the 1998 founding statement of bin Laden's and Zawahiri's "World Front". This war against the USA was justified by Washington's persistant inclination "to serve the Jew's petty state and divert attention from its occupation of Jerusalem and murder of Muslims there." As a result, killing Americans is "an individual duty for every Muslim ... in order to liberate the al-Aqsa Mosque and the holy mosque [Mecca] from their grip."[306] When in August 1998 the "World Front" blew up the American embassies in Kenya and Tanzania, this attack was also justified by "Israel's role in the tragedies which have befallen the Muslims ... Cooperation with the Israelis while they occupy the al-Aqsa Mosque amounts to a declaration of war against all Muslims throughout the world."[307]

Al-Qaʻida once again emphasized this anti-Israeli theme after September 11. Bin Laden ended his first videotape after the attack with the words, "I swear by God, that America will not live in peace until peace reigns in Palestine and all the armies of the unbelievers have left the land of Muhammad."[308] He reiterated this message in his second post-9/11 video. Terrorism against America, he declared "is praiseworthy, because it is an answer to injustice and is aimed at forcing America to end its support for Israel."[309] Thus, what was a central purpose of the September 11 attacks on the Pentagon and World Trade Centre? Bin Laden's answer could not have been clearer: "to force America to end its

306. The founding statement of the "World Front" can be found at www.fas.org/irp/world/para/docs/980223-fatwa.htm.
307. Bodansky, op. cit., pp. 292 and 231.
308. *Reuters*, October 7, 2001.
309. *NYT*, December 27, 2001.

support for Israel." Is it, therefore, any surprise that Islamists and their fellow travellers in all countries celebrated September 11?

The Antisemitic Signal

Even before September 11 bin Laden was regarded as a hero in the Islamic world. In 1989, after the withdrawal of the Red Army from Afghanistan, he toured Saudi Arabia in triumph. Over 250,000 cassettes of his speeches were legally sold and innumerable pirated copies distributed under the counter. The second wave of sympathy came in 1998. After al-Qaʻida had blown up the US embassies in Nairobi and Darussalam, killing over 250 people, the US struck back, firing 66 Cruise missiles at al-Qaʻida training camps in Afghanistan. By surviving the assault, bin Laden now achieved real cult status. Osama means "lion" and so the demonstrators now chanted, "Osama the Lion has come out of his cage to devour the enemies of Islam." The leader of Sudan's Islamists, Hassan al-Turabi, declared in 1998 that the Muslim youth saw him as their model: hatred of the USA would "create 10,000 bin Ladens."[310]

This cult has reached new levels of intensity since September 11. If bin Laden were indeed the architect of September 11, enthused the Egyptian columnist Salim Arrouz in the Islamist daily *Al-Ahrar*, "I will make a statue of him and set it in my home; I will also hang his picture in my office. Because he has proved to us that the USA ... can be humiliated." In the weekly magazine of the Egyptian Muslim Brotherhood, *Afaq Arabia*, a certain Dr Ahmad al-Magdoub wrote ecstatically, "Oh Osama ... you are a hero in the full sense of the word. [You possess] all the manly virtues, those [virtues] lacking in the half-men who control the Muslim and Arab resources."[311]

---

310. Bodansky, op. cit., pp. 28 and 295ff.
311. "The Egyptian Government, Opposition and Independent Press All Celebrate the Terrorist Attacks on the US," *MEMRI Special Dispatch*, no. 281, October 4, 2001.

September 11 was also greeted with storms of applause in the Palestinian Authority territories. The Islamists of Gaza were especially euphoric in their support. Over a dozen Hamas cadre had been trained in bin Laden's camps with Ahmed Yassin personally handing out the travel expenses to his organization's Afghanistan-bound militants.[312] The Palestinian Authority was repeatedly compelled to disperse pro-Osama meetings and demonstrations.[313] Things were little different on the West Bank. Immediately after news of the attacks arrived, 3,000 people flocked together in Nablus to express their joy with chants of "God is great."[314]

But how did the Islamic clergy respond to the religiously justified murders in New York? Sheikh Muhammad Sayed Tantawi, the head of Cairo's al-Azhar mosque, which has a decisive influence in Sunni Islam, did at least criticise the September 11 actions as "unislamic." Of greater significance, however, is the fact that no Islamic religious scholar anywhere in the world declared bin Laden an apostate for leading a terrorist organization. Nor was there any sign of a root-and-branch rejection of the concept of Islam put forward by bin Laden in his videos. Only in exceptional cases was the overdue call for a ban on suicide murders heard in the Islamic world.[315] When in April 2002, 54 Islamic states assembled in Malaysia for the Organization of Islamic Countries conference, the host's proposal that in future any attack on civilians should be designated a terrorist act was rejected. As if al-Banna's jihadism had taken over the Islamic world, there was almost unanimous support for Palestinian suicide murders at this gathering.[316]

312. Douglas Frantz, Chris Hedges, " Faintly Connected Dots Portray Al-Qaeda Man," *NYT*, January 11, 2002; Udo Ulfkotte, "Die Fäden des pan-islamischen Terrornetzes, *FAZ*, September 17, 2001; and Barsky, op. cit., pp. 5ff.
313. "Autonomiebehörde verhaftet Islamisten," *FAZ*, October 11, 2001.
314. *Hamburger Abendblatt*, September 12, 2001.
315. Douglas Jehl, "Speaking in the Name of Islam," *NYT*, December 2, 2001; Rainer Hermann, "Die Ich-Erzählung Gottes," *FAZ*, December 28, 2001.
316. "Verurteilung von Attentaten abgelehnt" *FAZ*, April 3, 2002.

But the European Union's reaction was scandalous as well. It would be "totally irresponsible," warned the French Ambassador to Israel, Jacques Huntzinger, setting the tone as early as September 14, 2001, "to compare the terrorist attack on the USA to the suicide bombings against Israelis, since the context is totally different."[317] Ambassador Huntzinger will have been informed that al-Qa'ida and Hamas stem from the same Qutbite tradition and are intertwined at the personal level. Are there nonetheless mitigating circumstances for Hamas' mass murders? Is there perhaps just that bit more European understanding for massacres when they affect Israeli Jews rather than the American superpower?

In any case, this approach facilitates European business with the Arab world. Only by totally separating al-Qa'ida and Hamas does it become possible for people to interpret Palestinian terror against Israeli civilians as an over-exuberant expression of some Palestinian "liberation struggle" and do business with its Iranian financiers with an untroubled conscience. The fact the PLO had asked the European Union to reward suicide bombers by letting their family members receive money from Brussels only came to light through a leak. In a wish list presented in April 2002, the Palestinian Planning Minister Nabil Shaath requested 20.6 million euros under the item "food and cash aid for the families of martyrs."[318] Although this was rejected, Brussels made it quite clear that Arafat could support the suicide bombing campaign and even finance it with EU money without any danger of forfeiting European support. Brussels dismissed all the warnings and information from Israel, with the result that "at least a hundred, perhaps several hundred members of various Fatah militia" who had taken part in terrorist attacks on Israeli civilians, "were at

317. "French Envoy Irritates Israel," *IHT*, September 15, 2001.
318. "Die PLO will, daß die EU Selbstmordattentate bezahlt," *Die Welt*, April 27, 2002.

the same time receiving European money for their work in [PA] security services."[319]

Instead of making the connection between the suicide attacks in Tel Aviv and those in Washington and New York, a causal link was cobbled together between the September 11 attacks and Israeli policies, which had allegedly "prepared the breeding-ground for terror" and were the starting point for the escalating "spiral of violence" leading up to the New York explosion. While in February 2002 Arafat's office received another 60 million euros without any political strings attached, the Europeans attacked Israel for conducting that very same "war against terror" in which, at least verbally, they were standing side-by-side with the American administration.[320]

Thus, the acclaim with which the Islamic states greeted the suicide bombings in Palestine and Europe's attitude of benevolent understanding of them gave rise to a most paradoxical situation: as if some al-Qa'ida director were secretly running the global theatre of mass psychology, September 11 boomeranged back onto, of all countries, Israel.

Sometimes, the Jewish state was even held directly responsible for September 11. The legend, invented and circulated by the Hizbullah television station, *Al Manar*, that, following warnings from the Israeli secret service agency Mossad, 4,000 Jews had not gone to work at the World Trade Centre on September 11, reached untold millions around the world with lightning speed. "Hey USA!!! Why 4,000 Jews Can Escape from Boom?" became the watchword in the Islamic world.

---

319.   Yoel Esteron, "Europe Finally Wakes Up and Recognizes Arafat's Nastiness," *IHT*, December 14, 2001; Thomas Kleine-Brockhoff, Unbeugsame Gutgläubigkeit, *Die Zeit*, August 15, 2002.
320.   *Deutsche Presseagentur*, February 26, 2002; "EU Hilft Palästinensern mit Millionen-Finanzspritze," *NZZ*, April 25, 2002; "Scharfe Verurteilung Israels durch den Europarat," *FAZ*, April 15, 2002. "Scharping: keine Rüstungsexporte."

What picture of "the Jews" does this story paint? Firstly it accepts the legend that Mossad will stop at nothing to damage the Arab states. Secondly, it suggests that every Jew outside of Israel will at the crucial moment obey orders from Tel Aviv with military discipline. Thirdly it assumes the existence of a will to destroy the non-Jewish population, since, according to the legend, New York Jews cold-bloodedly left their non-Jewish colleagues to die. Goebbel's rule that a lie only has to be monstrous enough to be believed is here faithfully followed. This hate-virus against Jews was disseminated worldwide across the Internet to untold millions. The global spread and acceptance of this message in itself marks a watershed. Overnight, the fabrication of a Jewish world conspiracy had gained widespread currency as the basic interpretative framework for an event of global significance.

While September 11 drove not only Israel, but also many Jewish communities in Europe into unexpected political isolation, for the anti-Semites of Europe and the Arab world it served as a signal announcing the reawakening of antisemitism in its new globalized form.

Let us begin with the Arab world, where in spring 2002 the jihad escalated in a way that would have been unthinkable before September 11. The stimulus came from the situation in the Palestinian Authority territories, where the intifada and the attack had strengthened Hamas. While opinion polls showed support for the PLO falling from 33% to 20% between October 2000 and October 2002, the popularity of Hamas rose from 23% to 31%. In the first elections to a student representative body after September 11, in Nablus University, Hamas won 60% of the vote, way ahead of Fatah with 34%.[321]

At the same time the wave of acclaim for the Palestinian suicide bombers swelled unchecked. Thus in December 2001

321. Jane Bennet, "In Hamas, a Rising Peril to Arafat," *IHT*, December 7, 2001.

the Arafat-appointed Mufti of Jerusalem, Sheikh Ikrama Sabri, expressed his support "for suicide attacks more clearly than ever before." And, while at that time the highest Sunni religious author-ity, the Al-Azhar Mosque's Sheikh Muhammad Sayed Tantawi, was still condemning these attacks in a *fatwa*, a few months later this hurdle too was passed. In April 2002 Tantawi announced that "every martyrdom operation against any Israeli, including children, women, and teenagers, is a legitimate act according to [Islamic] religious law, and an Islamic commandment, until the people of Palestine regain their land and cause the cruel Israeli aggression to retreat."[322] Abandoning the speech code previously followed by Arafat, Palestinian Authority officials now began openly advocating suicide murders, while the PFLP started glo-rifying "love of martyrdom" as a "divine weapon."[323] Finally, in a "Letter from al-Qa'ida to the Muslims and the Heroic Palestin-ian People," Osama bin Laden himself added his voice, linking the attacks in Israel and New York and praising them as "great achievements" and "blessed holy war."[324]

And so Palestinian society in the spring of 2002 began to turn itself in reality into that "industry of death" for which Has-san al-Banna had yearned in 1936. The mass murder of Jewish civilians had become accepted as a self-evident ideal for the aver-age Palestinian. Hamas' antisemitic program was being put into eliminatory practice.

A macabre unreal world: in the Gaza strip 700 of 1,000 youngsters polled stated that they wished to blow themselves up in jihad. Hamas sold videos explaining how to make a do-it-yourself suicide bomber's belt. Pre-school children were rehearsed for jihad through children's TV programs presenting suicide attacks in cartoon form. And in the surreal valedictory

---

322. Cited in *MEMRI Special Dispatch*, no. 363, April 7, 2002.
323. Joseph Croitoru, "Israel und der Medienkrieg," *FAZ*, April 12, 2002, and *Nahost Focus*, June 5, 2002.
324. *NZZ*, March 29, 2002.

films of the young mass murderers their mothers increasingly appeared, not hopelessly or despairingly, but proudly and joyfully extolling the sacrifice of their sons not in the act of saving but of killing others.

When out of necessity the Israeli government took military countermeasures, the Islamists' calculations were realized: antisemitic fury gripped the Arab world. For weeks on end pictures from Jenin and elsewhere - technically perfect but torn totally from their political context – were transmitted as a burning call to action over the Arab News Network (ANN) and Hizbullah's Al-Manar TV to every Arab household; no words, just pictures accompanied by martial music.[325] The Israeli military actions were unscrupulously separated from their context – the murderous frenzy of the suicide bombers – in order to project Hamas' own eliminatory methods onto their victims, the Jews. At the same time other governments further fuelled the suicide war against Israel.

Iraq, for example, in April 2002 raised its payments to suicide bombers' families from 10,000 to 25,000 dollars and promised the Palestinians special assistance to the tune of 8.7 million dollars. Saddam Hussein sent greetings to the Palestinian suicide murderers, in particular to the "brave women who bid farewell to their sons full of satisfaction at their self-sacrifice, carried out in order to terrify and drive to despair the Zionist and American powers."[326]

In *Saudi Arabia* the state controlled newspaper *Al-Watan* published a two-part article on the "hellish plan of the Jews to take over the world." The spirit of eliminatory antisemitism was further whipped up in sermons from Mecca and Medina broadcast on Saudi state television. On April 19, 2002, the prayer went

325. Thomas L. Friedmann, "Global Village Idiocy," *NYT*, May 12, 2002.
326. Philip Smucker and Nicholas Blanford, "Arab States Vent Rising Wrath," *Christian Science Monitor*, April 22, 2002; Hussain al-Mozany, "Tarife für Gotteskrieger," *FAZ*, July 26, 2002.

up in Medina for Allah to "destroy the Jews, scatter them, annihilate them soon, and have mercy on our brothers and sisters
in Palestine. Help our oppressed brothers in Chechnya, Kash-
mir and elsewhere," while the lesson from the Mecca Mosque
was that "the Jews of yesterday were bad ancestors and those of
today are worse descendants. They are the scum of the earth.
Allah hurled curses at them and turned them into apes and pigs
and worshippers of tyrants. This is what the Jews are: a constant
source of viciousness, division, wilfulness, tyranny, malice and
corruption."[327]

Finally, in *Iran*, the supreme religious authority, Ayatollah
Khamenei, called a "World Conference to Support the Intifada," at which the suicide murderer, as the "highest expression
of courage, honour and worth of a nation," was contrasted to
the "cancer" of Israel, which must be obliterated, and warnings
issued against the "Israeli-American trap" of "pushing the Palestinians into new talks."[328]

Taking up precisely this demand – "no talks" – massive demonstrations in support of the suicide intifada took place in all the
major Arab cities in spring 2002, often organized by the Muslim Brothers. A million marched in Rabat (Morocco), 300,000
in Sanaa (Yemen) and Khartoum (Sudan), 100,000 in Tripoli
(Libya), Cairo and Baghdad and 20,000 in Amman (Jordan) and
the Gulf Emirate of Bahrain. "Bin Laden, bin Laden, hit Tel Aviv,"
shouted the crowd in Amman. "The army of Muhammad will
return, the army of Muhammad is already at the border!" was
another slogan. Here the Jordanian Muslim Brothers were the
main organized force.[329] In Egypt the main demand of the five

327. "Saudi Government Daily: the Jews are Taking Over the World", *MEM-
RI Special Dispatch*, no. 321, December 28, 2001 and "Saudi Government TV
Broadcasts Sermon Calling to Annihilate the Jews 'Annihilate them Soon'",
Middle East Report of the Foreign Broadcast Information Service (FBIS), April
19, 2002.
328. *Nahost Focus*, June 5, 2002.
329. Neil MacFarquhar, "Cairo Conference Demands International Action
against Israel," *NYT*, March 9, 2002; "Anger in the Streets is Exerting Pressure

consecutive daily mass demonstrations was for "permission for Egyptians to join the armed struggle of the Palestinians against the Israeli occupying power." The same demand was made in an appeal signed by Islamists from 20 countries, including groups from South Africa, Nigeria, Sudan and Bangladesh, as well as Hamas, Hizbullah and the Turkish Islamist Erbakan.[330] So here it was, the Muslim mass movement summoned up the signal of September 11. Six months after the fall of the World Trade Centre, in anticipation of further massacres, the greatest festival of eliminatory antisemitism since 1945 took place.

It was not the USA's war against the Taliban that brought the Islamic masses onto the streets, but Hamas' offensive against Israel's very existence. The good mood at this jihad party was buoyed up not only by the millions on the streets of the Arab capitals, but also by the solidarity actions taking place in Europe. Here, the attack on the World Trade Centre electrified the Nazi milieu and breathed new life into the historic alliance between the Mufti and the Führer.

New Alliances

"The alliance is formed," declared the Nazi and Muslim convert Ahmed Huber, who had had several meetings with al-Qa'ida militants. "11 September brought both sides together, because the bulk of the new right responded positively to the attacks."[331] These forces had indeed hailed September 11 as an assault on "Jewish-plutocratic Wall Street" and the heart of the "Zionist Occupation Government."[332] As Horst Mahler, the former spokesman of the German Nazi party, the NPD, explained admiringly, "After Arafat's betrayal of his people the initiative in the struggle against

on Arab Moderates," *NYT*, April 3, 2002.
330. "Heiliger Krieg gegen Israel," *taz*, April 11, 2002.
331. Peter Finn, "Joined in Mutual Hate, Europe's Fringe Right Courts Muslims", *IHT*, April 30, 2002.
332. From the homepage of White Power MP3, cited in K. Eschrich, "Ein Feind, ein guter Feind", *Jungle World*, December 19, 2001.

Jewish domination passed to the Islamic holy warriors," ushering in "the decade of the defeat of the Judeo-American Empire."[333] A "National and Social Action Alliance of West Thuringia" drew the conclusions, explaining that the Islamists of Hamas and Islamic Jihad were the natural allies in the struggle against the "US terrorists" and their "commanders" in Israel, deemed the real "secret world government."[334] They therefore added their voice to Mahler's call for a "global intifada" against the "agents of Jewish power."[335]

Global intifada! This slogan also caught on among left-wing anti-globalists, especially in Italy, and it was through this channel that it first gripped masses of people and made a real political impact. Organized by the Italian anti-globalization movement, the Western world's biggest demonstration to date in support of the suicide intifada in Palestine took place on March 9, 2002 – at almost the same time as the upsurge of jihadism in the Arab world – as 100,000 marched in the Italian capital Rome.

Preparations for this demonstration had begun immediately after September 11. Press reports that this demonstration wished to take its cue from both Zionist and Palestinian violence were angrily rebutted by one of the organizers of the "anti-imperialist camp." The march, he insisted, had a "clearly anti-imperialist character," since it demanded the release by the Palestinian Authority of all "militants of the intifada" and defended the right of the Palestinians "to use any means they consider appropriate for the liberation of Palestine."[336]

It was at precisely this time – March 2002 – that the escalation of suicide murder attacks in Israel reached their high point. While previously the left had correctly defined massacres

---

333. Horst Mahler, "Heil Juda! Wir kommen!", *Netzsplitter*, June 18, 2002.
334. *Der Rechte Rand* no. 73, Nov/Dec. 2001, p. 4.
335. Alfred Schobert, "Im Haß auf Israel vereint", *Allgemeine Jüdische Wochenzeitung*, October 11, 2001.
336. "Support the New Intifada!", statement by the Anti-Imperialist Camp of June 2001.

of civilians, as in Brescia, Italy in 1974 or at the Munich *Okto-berfest* in 1980, as fascist in character, the monstrous was now accepted as normal. Worse still, while the escalation in suicide bombings should have led to a strengthening of solidarity with the predominantly Jewish victims and a withdrawal of support from the attacks' organizers, this particular left did exactly the opposite: the more indiscriminately the Palestinian commandos killed Israeli civilians, the more frenetic the "anti-imperialist" applause for the intifada. But what have fascist and anti-imperialist anti-globalization movements to do with the Islamism they praise or defend? The answer has to do with the political turning point of 1989/1990.

Although the communist ideal as an alternative to capitalism had lain in ruins at least since Stalin's time, it was only this turning point that led to its total disappearance. Since, however, the state of the world did not thereafter change for the better, the collapse of the communist utopia set in motion a search for attractive "anti-capitalist" ersatz ideologies. For the time being, the winner of this unregulated competition is the anti-globalization movement.

As a rule, however, this movement fails to analyze the totality of a capitalist world in which a little shop in Mogadishu and a multinational company in the USA are caught up in the same logic. Instead, it arbitrarily seizes on specific aspects of capitalism - the stock market, for instance, or "Wall Street," "finance capital," or "the USA" – removes them from their context and mistakenly holds them responsible for all the evils allegedly produced by the logic of capitalism. So instead of recognising that the concrete and abstract aspects of the market economy are intertwined, these aspects are sorted into two categories and divided into a good (concrete) and an evil (abstract) principle.

This analysis of capitalism is a romantic one, motivated by the hope that by isolating and fighting the so-called abstract elements of capitalism one can create a more "natural" and "organic" kind of community. Any movement, however, which tends to personalize such artificially separated elements of the economy runs the risk of consciously or unconsciously resorting to the antisemitic stereotypes by identifying "money" and "money power" with the "Jews." This is why today's Nazis are fond of anti-globalism. Indeed, for many years the German Nazi youth organization has lurked behind the website www.gegen-globalisierung.de.

As part of its strategy, al-Qa'ida also attempts to align its slogans with those of the anti-globalization movement. Abu Ubeid al-Qurashi, identified by several Arabic newspapers as one of Osama bin Laden's closest aides, explained this in a statement of principles published in February 2002, which states that the Islamic movement "must increase interest in *Da'wa* [proselytising], and recruit the peoples' public and political support... Old strategists, such as [von] Clausewitz and Mao Zedong, have already indicated this." In an article published four weeks later al-Qurashi spelt out what the focus of these efforts should be: "The Islamic nation is struggling against globalization, and it continues with its negative attitude towards Western rhetoric and explanations." [337]

In spring 2002, for the first time this reactionary, conspiracy theory-fuelled kind of anti-capitalism showed its true face in Europe too. Just as the new surge in jihadism was shaking the Arab world, Europe experienced the worst outbreak of antisemitic violence since the *Kristallnacht* pogrom of 1938.

In France the previously silent islamization of the poor neighbourhoods by Saudi-financed Imams ("*la benladenization des banlieues*") gave way to a wave of antisemitic attacks. Jewish schools and synagogues were set on fire and Jewish cemeteries

---

337. "Bin Laden Lieutenant Admits to September 11 and Explains Al-Qa'ida's Combat Doctrine," *MEMRI Special Dispatch*, no. 344, February 10, 2002; "Al-Qa'ida Activist, Abu Ubeid al-Qurashi: Comparing Munich (Olympics) Attacks to September 11," *MEMRI Special Dispatch*, no. 353, March 12, 2002.

desecrated. The White Paper *Les Antijuifs* records over four hundred violent criminal acts against persons. The scope of the wave of assaults that began at the same time as the intifada in September 2000 widened noticeably after September 11. In Brussels Jewish businesses were set alight and Molotov cocktails thrown at synagogues.[338] In Italy the number of attacks on Jewish targets rose and in Germany antisemitism became a vote-catcher and so for the first time a real force in the political mainstream. In April 2002 a representative survey found that 20% of Germans considered the Jews responsible for the major conflicts in the world. In 2003 an opinion poll conducted for the European Commission revealed an even more frightening mood. Offered a simple yes or no response to the question of whether certain countries threatened world peace, 59% of Europeans answered in the affirmative about Israel – placing it at the top of a list that included, among others, Afghanistan, Iraq, Syria, Iran and Pakistan.[339]

How stubbornly rooted the fantasy that makes the Jews the all-purpose scapegoat has become was demonstrated by leading French anti-globalization activist, José Bové. Famous for having destroyed a McDonalds restaurant, Bové, who currently enjoys a certain renown as the unofficial leader not only of the younger generation of French leftwingers, but also of the international anti-globalization movement, intuitively knew who was behind the wave of antisemitic attacks in France. On the French TV channel Canal Plus he stated that, "the attacks on the French synagogues are either orchestrated or carried out by Mossad."[340]

Massive anti-Jewish upsurges in the Arab world and Europe: al-Qaʿida, which had banked on such after-shocks, could feel sat-

---

338. Jurg Altwegg, "Intifada in Paris," *FAZ*, March 14, 2002; Michael Meyer-Resende, "Kritik an Israel wird oft nur als Vorwand benutzt," *Berliner Zeitung*, March 16, 2002; "Jüdische Geschäfte in Brüssel ausgebrannt," *NZZ*, April 18, 2002.
339. Philip Carmel, Israel, long wary of European bias, seemingly finds confirmation in poll, in: *JTA*, November 5, 2003.
340. Christopher Caldwell, "Liberté, Egalité, Judeophobie", *Weekly Standard*, vol. 7, no. 33, June 5, 2002.

isfied by this response to September 11. In assessments of the September attacks it laid special stress on their trigger effect. The massacre had been a "propaganda record-breaker" for Islamism an al-Qaʻida spokesman emphasized. "With few exceptions, the entire planet heard about it." The New York attack "rang the bells of restoring Arab and Islamic glory."[341]

Even if this may strike us as somewhat exaggerated, it is certainly the case that Islamism's death-knell is yet to toll. Admittedly, the American military strikes have destroyed the jihadist infrastructure in Afghanistan and forced the al-Qaʻida cadre into hiding. As yet however, there has been no long-lasting political success in stemming the forward march of jihadism in the Islamic world. Post-September 11, antisemitism, rather than being proscribed and marginalized, has become a globally potent force. Whoever does not want to combat antisemitism, however, hasn't the slightest chance of beating Islamism.

Our review of the conditions which give rise to modern jihadism has shown that from the start it has been inextricably bound up with the hatred of Jews. This is not self-explanatory. The effects of British colonialist policies and capitalist crisis at the end of the 1920s fostered the emergence of Islamism as a movement of resistance to modernity and provoked the appeal for a return to a new sharia-based order. Nevertheless, the Muslim Brothers' call to jihad was almost exclusively targeted on Zionism and the Jews: the Muslim Brotherhood became a mass organization not as an anti-colonial but as an anti-Jewish movement.[342] Jihadism did not merely spur this antisemitism; it was constituted by it.

---

341. "Al-Qaʼida Activist, Abu Ubeid al-Qurashi: Comparing Munich (Olympics) Attacks to September 11", *MEMRI Special Dispatch*, no. 353, March 12, 2002; "Bin Laden Lieutenant Admits to September 11 and Explains Al-Qaʼida's Combat Doctrine", *MEMRI Special Dispatch*, no. 344, February 10, 2002
342. The exception confirming this rule was provided at the end of 1951 when the Egyptian Prime Minister, Nahhas Pasha unilaterally ratified the Anglo-Egyptian cooperation treaty. Immediately afterwards the Muslim

The *ikhwan*'s Jew-hatred, which erupted into the demonstrations and pogroms of 1936-39, 1945 and 1947-48 was fuelled by the anti-Jewish passages in the Koran and by Nazi antisemitism and anti-Zionism. It was the fusion of these different and independent sources that gave the anti-Jewish campaigns in Egypt their potency.

Why was it then that, unlike all the other semi-fascist movements of the 1930s, jihadism did not depart the stage of history after the defeat of the Nazis? How, despite the uncovering of the Shoah, could the Muslim Brothers' Jew-hatred survive the turning point of 1945 and, with Sayyid Qutb's antisemitic tract, even gain in venom? The answer has to do with the pro-Arab opportunism of the great powers after the war. All the victors of the Second World War contributed in one way or another to Amin el-Husseini's rehabilitation. Let us begin with the Western allies: in France, the war criminal was allowed to live like an official guest. Britain meekly withdrew its extradition request in response to objections from the Arab League. After the Mufti's flight to Egypt, the USA, which had previously insisted on his punishment, let the matter drop as well. Simon Wiesenthal hit the mark when in 1947 he compared the Mufti to an "unexploded bomb," "which people avoid because they haven't yet found the expert able to defuse and render it harmless for those around it." Addressing the Allies, Wiesenthal added that, "none of the governments has to this day ventured to call a spade a spade."[343]

The most important boost to the advance of Islamism was therefore given between 1945 and 1948. The victorious powers considered their good relations with the Arab world more important than countering the ideological concoction of antisemitism, Hitler-worship, Holocaust denial and the unbridled desire to destroy Israel, of which the Mufti was the supreme exponent. The

Brothers declared jihad against British troops stationed in the Canal Zone. See Mitchell, op. cit., pp. 88ff.
343. Wiesenthal, op. cit., p. 1.

consequences of this choice of priorities can scarcely be exaggerated. When the international community granted amnesty to the Mufti, much of the Arab world perceived this as the rehabilitation of National Socialism and antisemitism. Even when countless Nazi fugitives and the semi-official circulation of the *Protocols of the Elders of Zion* followed the Mufti to Egypt, the Allies again refused to "call a spade a spade." Although Nazi Germany had been defeated as a political adversary, its antisemitic ideology survived the Second World War relatively unscathed.

The foreign policy pursued by the Soviet Union since the mid-1950s was little different. There was no talk about the rejection of Arab anti-Zionism once expressed by the Soviet foreign minister to the United Nations. The Kremlin found it could come to terms with Nasser's Holocaust denial and antisemitic fervour.

When Nasser failed in his goal to destroy Israel in 1967 and the renaissance of Islamism began, it no longer had any need of a Nazi big brother state in Germany to foster its development. Anti-Zionism based on the *Protocols* of *the Elders of Zion* had long since found a new home in the Arab world, rooting itself especially firmly in Egypt.

However, it was not until the 1990s that Islamism for the first time became a global force. While, for example, at the height of the African independence movements in the 1960s Islam played no role even in West African countries with Muslim majorities, now Islamist influence expanded in Sudan, Nigeria and Somalia. While until 1990 the Soviet camp was the most significant opponent of capitalism, Islamism now began to take its place and translate the "critique" of capitalism into antisemitic terms.

The new anti-Jewish war could now start. In Palestine – the frontline in the struggle against "international Jewry" – it was heralded at the end of the 1980s by the foundation of Hamas and the successful launch of its Charter in 1988. 1993 saw the start of a series of suicidal mass murders through which the Palestinian Muslim Brothers advertised themselves as the vanguard of the jihad for the destruction of Israel. With 9/11, Islamism also established itself as the leading force amongst the supporters of Judeophobic anti-Americanism.

When Islamists label Israel as "really an American" and the USA as "really a Jewish" power, they can count on the support of anti-globalists of both left and right as well as the benevolent toleration of member states of the European Union. And so today's anti-Americanism and anti-Israelism are breathing new life into the reactionary antisemitic "critique of capitalism" central to the fascist and Nazi ideologies.

At the same time the main European powers' tacit acceptance of Arab antisemitism has taken on a new quality. Obviously, in the competition over the shaping of the future world order some European powers, such as Germany and France, seem determined to keep the centres of Islamism on their side at all costs. When in February 2002 the Iranian government refused to accept a new British ambassador on the sole grounds that he was Jewish, the German government let not a word of criticism publicly pass its lips.[344] And so the advance of Islamism is allowed to continue.

Jihad and Jew-hatred belong together. Approval of antisemitism strengthens jihadist barbarism. Any variety of anti-capitalism that wittingly or unwittingly has recourse to antisemitic forms of thought strengthens jihadism as well.

The struggle against jihadism therefore requires zero tolerance for antisemitism. Were Jew-hatred to be ostracized, isolated, prosecuted and punished on a global scale, then jihadism would be a thing of the past.

While the mills of Islamism may grind slowly, the goal is never lost from sight: the primary target of all the contemporary attacks is Israel. Former Hamas leader Ahmed Yassin held that 2027 would be the year of Israel's destruction. For him, 40 years

---

344. "Teheran lehnt britischen Botschafter ab," *FAZ*, February 11, 2002.

after the beginning of the intifada and the founding of Hamas the refuge of the Jewish people was scheduled to vanish from the map. Some oil states such as Iran agree with this perspective. Millions of Muslims, whipped up by the Muslim Brotherhood's propaganda, applaud. This lends urgency to the concern that something comparable to Auschwitz could happen again.

However, it is not only Israel that is at stake in the conflicts that lie ahead. Today, Israel is a symbol of otherness and difference. The contrary concept is that of forced homogeneity. Any commitment to a society that seeks to foster the emancipation of the individual requires a categorical rejection of the Islamist ideal of homogeneity. Israel is no better than other countries, but the outcome of the battle for its secure existence will determine the future of the world.

"The victory of the Zionist idea is the turning point for the fulfilment of an ideal which is so dear to me, the revival of the Orient," the Egyptian politician Ahmed Zaki declared eighty-five years ago on the fifth anniversary of the Balfour Declaration. Because this hope has been dashed, Zaki's words today take on a new meaning: recognition and defence of the Jewish state or Islamist barbarism – this is the "turning point" which confronts humanity at this moment in history.

EPILOGUE
. . . .
"...THE BEGINNING OF COMPLICITY."

The destruction of the Twin Towers of the World Trade Center triggered an unprecedented wave of anti-Jewish madness - since 11 September there have been more antisemites and more antisemitism than ever before in the world. Among the more spectacular expressions of this development are:

-   In Egypt in 2002 the *Protocols of the Elders of Zion* - the work that Hitler took as his guide for the Holocaust - was made into a 41-part television series. This was broadcast during Ramadan in Egypt and then sold on to at least 17 other Islamic TV channels. In the view of antisemitism expert Robert Wistrich, the demonisation of the Jews in this series, produced for a mass audience, reaches an intensity that surpasses that of even the Nazis' antisemitic films.[345]

-   In 2003 another *Protocols*-based TV series, this time in 29 parts, was produced by Syria and Hezbollah. In one episode the ritual murder of a young Christian boy by two Jews is presented in close-up. Any child viewing this scene of slaughter might be damaged for the rest of his or her life. It will take generations to extract this mental poison.

-   In the same year the retiring Malaysian Prime Minister, Dato Seri Mahathir, opened a global Islamic conference in Kuala Lumpur with a speech attacking "the Jews" as

345. According to Professor Wistrich in his talk at the Global Forum for Combating Antisemitism held in Jerusalem on February 12, 2007.

the deceitful rulers of the world. The representatives of 57 states greeted this outburst with a standing ovation. Not one leader from the Islamic world disassociated him or herself from Mahathir's remarks. Mahathir is known as an opponent of the Islamists. This scene demonstrates not only that the Islamists' antisemitism meets no resistance in the Muslim *umma*, but that Jew-hatred is increasingly becoming its most important common denominator.

- At the beginning of 2006 a majority of Palestinian Arabs voted for Hamas in democratic elections, thus putting into government a group whose worldview is based on the *Protocols*.

- In Egypt, Jordan and Syria, the force most likely to gain power in the event of democratic elections is the Muslim Brotherhood whose leaders agree with Iran's president Mahmoud Ahmadinejad in denying the Holocaust and calling for the destruction of Israel.

- Since 1979 Iran has become one of the world's most important sources of antisemitic films and books. Since Mahmud Ahmadinejad was elected President, Iran has further radicalised in this direction. It has made Holocaust denial the centrepiece of its foreign policy - not in order to revise the past, but to shape the future, by preparing for a new Holocaust in the form of the loudly proclaimed destruction of Israel.

This tsunami of madness is only indirectly connected to the anti-Jewish passages in the core Islamic texts. The aim of the mediaeval hatred of Jews (and Christians) in the Islamic world was to keep the *dhimmis* down or push them to convert. Hostility towards the Jews was connected to their debasement. The "eliminatory antisemitism" (to use Daniel J. Goldhagen's term) prevalent today over-estimates rather than under-estimates Jews. Now, as "the rulers of the world", they are deemed responsible for all misfortunes, and this leaves only one way out: to save the world by eradicating them. "The extermination of Jewry throughout the world", declared a Nazi directive from 1943, is "the precondition for an enduring peace."[346] This is similar to the mission that Islamism has set out upon whose first target is Israel. As Mahmud Ahmadinejad put it, "The Zionist regime will be wiped out and humanity will be liberated."[347] The shocking malice of such words leads people to suppress them or block them out. "We instinctively look away, as we do whenever we are confronted with monstrous deformity," writes David Gelernter. "Nothing is harder or more frightening to look at than a fellow human who is bent out of shape."[348]

But while this may to some extent excuse the attitude of the ordinary citizen, it cannot justify the way the media and the politicians have been behaving. Knowing the historical consequences of "redemptive antisemitism" (Saul Friedländer), they ought to be on red alert. Instead they have shut their eyes. The fact that since 11 September Jew-hatred has reached truly epidemic proportions in the Islamic world has been downplayed or ignored.

In 2003 the European Union had dealt with the issue of Mahathir's antisemitic speech - coincidentally the EU's Heads of State and Government were gathering for a summit on the day after it was made. A condemnation of Mahathir was prepared for the concluding document, but the French and Greek leaders Chirac and Simitis wielded their veto and got the criticism of Mahathir's antisemitism shunted into a siding. Mahathir later publicly thanked Chirac for his initiative.

When in 2004 the Organization for Security and Co-operation in Europe (OSCE) held a major conference in Berlin

346. Herf, op .cit., p. 209.
347. Yigal Carmon, 'The Role of Holocaust Denial in the Ideology and Strategy of The Iranian Regime', *The Middle East Media Research Institute (MEMRI), Inquiry and Analysis Series*, No. 307, December 15, 2006.
348. David Gelernter, Beyond Barbarism in the Middle East, *Jewish World Review*, March 19, 2002.

to combat antisemitism, the French delegate Pierre Lellouche pointed the right way forward with a proposal that similar conferences should in the future be held in Cairo or Amman. But the next speaker, German foreign minister Joschka Fischer, immediately swept the proposal off the table, arguing that antisemitism was a European problem, "not one for other countries and cultures". And indeed, as a result of pressure from not only Arab, but also European countries, the conference's final document makes no mention of Islamic antisemitism.[349]

In 2005 not only the EU, but also the USA greeted Hamas' participation in the elections, without considering the fact that the organisation's programme, its Charter, "sounds as if it were copied out from the pages of *Der Stürmer*", as Sari Nusseibeh, the former PLO representative in Jerusalem accurately observed.[350] The fact that Hamas would not have been permitted to stand in elections on this antisemitic programme in any European country was ignored.

The specific danger presented by the Iranian nuclear programme is rarely addressed. It arises out of the unique ideological stew of which it is an ingredient: that mish-mash of antisemitism and weapons-grade uranium, Holocaust denial and high-tech, death cult and missile research, Shiite messianism and plutonium. Here the worst case scenario is not an increase in suicide bombing attacks against individuals, but a suicide nuking of the Israeli state. However, in the UN Security Council decisions and the positions of the Permanent Five, the technical dimension of Iran's nuclear programme is as a rule divorced from its ideological background.

Islamic antisemitism is a taboo subject even in some parts of academia. Professor Pieter von der Horst from the University

---

349. Toby Axelrod, 'Conference in Berlin condemns anti-Semitism, calls for monitoring', *JTA*, April 29, 2004; 'Man musste klar reden', Interview with Yehuda Bauer, *taz*, April 30, 2004.
350. From Leon Wieselthier, 'Sympathy for the Other', *New York Times Book Review*, April 1, 2007.

of Utrecht in the Netherlands found this out when, after 37 years of teaching, he proposed to give his valedictory lecture on the topic of the anti-Jewish blood libel. The head of the university asked him to excise the section of his lecture dealing with Islamic antisemitism. When he refused to do so, he was invited to appear before a panel of four professors who insisted he remove these passages. A lecture on Islamic antisemitism, so the argument went, might lead to violent reactions from well-organised Muslim student groups. Moreover such a lecture would complicate the intercultural dialogue. Von der Horst saw no other way forward than to accede to this pressure. Nonetheless the complete version of his lecture subsequently reached a wide audience in the Netherlands and beyond.

Similar things have happened to me. When in April 2003 I was invited by Yale University as keynote speaker on the topic of "Islamic Terrorism and Antisemitism: The Mission against Modernity", there was such a storm of protest that the organisers changed the program. The original title of one of the panels - "Islamic Jihad. A Case of Global Non-State Terrorism" - was changed to "Global, Non-State Terrorism". In addition a speaker was added to the podium whose sole qualification was that of being President of the local "Palestine Right to Return Coalition". At least I was able to give my talk. Not so four years later at the University of Leeds in Britain. Here too the collocation "Islamic antisemitism" acted like a red rag to a bull. Following e-mail protests by two Muslim students, my lecture title "Hitler's Legacy: Islamic antisemitism in the Middle East" was changed to "The Nazi Legacy: Export of Antisemitism into the Middle East". In vain! On the day of my arrival in Leeds, the University administration cancelled my talk "on security grounds". No one, including the Muslim students, had threatened violence. As before in Utrecht, freedom of speech was suspended by an act of preemptive self-censorship.[351]

Both university administrations clearly believed they were meeting the wishes of their numerous Muslim students in suspending freedom of speech and forbidding mention of a real problem in the lecture halls.

The absurdity of this behaviour, however, becomes clear when we realise that Muslims themselves have been criticizing Islamic antisemitism. Following the fall of Saddam Hussein statements by Muslims arguing for a reform of Islam have mushroomed. Since examples of intra-religious criticism of antisemitism remain rare, they deserve a hearing for this very reason.

- "Why do we hate the Jews?" asked Saudi columnist Hussein Shubakshi in the London-based Arabic daily *Al-Sharq Al-Awsat* in May 2005. "The extent of the tremendous hatred of the Jews is baffling. ... If we know ... the true reason why the Jews have become the reason for every catastrophe, then we will be able to understand the idea of dividing [human beings] into groups."

- In January 2006 Tunisian Philosopher Mezri Haddad complained that Arab public opinion "has found in antisemitism the perfect catalyst for all its narcissistic wounds and social, economic, and political frustrations." The fundamentalist had, to be sure "reduced the Koran to a case of nauseating antisemitism," but it must be admitted, "that some Koranic verses, intentionally isolated from their historical context, have contributed even more to the anchoring of antisemitic stereotypes in Arab-Muslim mentalities". This "petrifaction" of the Arab-Muslim mentality can be reversed, but this would require "intel-

---

351. Matthias Küntzel, "Is there no longer room for debate?," The Times Higher Education Supplement, March 23, 2007. I was later re-invited by the Vice-Chancellor of Leeds University and will hopefully deliver my lecture in October 2007.

lectual audacity" on the part of Islamic scholars. "Since they cannot purge the Koran of its potentially antisemitic dross, they must closely examine this corpus with hermeneutical reasoning."

- In April 2007 Egyptian author Hisham al-Tuhi recalled the role that the Jews played "in the Egyptian renaissance (*nahdha*)" of the 1920s: "[Jews] founded the Salt and Soda Company... the Egyptian Petrol company... the Rice-hulling Company... the Egyptian Real Estate Bank... the Family Bank... In the arts they were creators and performers who took part in the revival of music and singing and in the launch of Egyptian cinema and theatre." He commented on the expulsions of the Arab Jews since the 1950s and the fact that Jews are denigrated "with the ugliest abuse in the prayers of the Muslims, in all of the Arab mosques" and depicted as infidels, accursed souls and traitors "in the books, the newspapers, and the TV stations, [both] governmental and private", and wished the tiny handful of Jews still remaining in Egypt precisely for that reason a "Happy Passover".[352]

So while some Muslims support the universal struggle against antisemitism and in so doing are making an invaluable contribution to a peaceful solution in the Middle East, other Muslims want to prevent any mention, let along any public discussion, of Islamic antisemitism. It is the latter group that has profited from the actions of Utrecht and Leeds Universities.

No wonder then that an increasing number of anti-Islamist Muslims are complaining about the "well-meaning" behaviour of Western academics. "When Westerners make politically-correct

---

352. *On the Saudi columnist in Al-Sharq Al-Awsat, see 'We Must Discuss Why We Hate The Jews',* MEMRI, *Special Dispatch* No. 913, May 27, 2005. On Haddad: 'Tunisian Philosopher Mezri Haddad: Islamists have reduced the Koran to a Nauseating Antisemitic Lampoon', MEMRI, *Special Dispatch Series* No. 1362, 21 November 2006; on Hisham al-Tuhi: 'To the Arab Jews: Happy Passover!' www.*MEMRI.org*, April 24, 2007.

excuses for Islamism, it actually endangers the lives of reformers and in many cases has the effect of suppressing their voices,"
argues Tawfik Hamid, a former member of the Egyptian Islamist
organisation Gama'a al-Islamiyya.

These Western colleagues, according to Hamid, with their
political correctness, "prevent any clear criticism of sharia law
which, for example, exhorts good Muslims to exterminate the
Jews before the 'end of the days'".

Hamid concludes by remarking that, "without confronting
the ideological roots of Islamism, it will be impossible to combat it"[353] - a reality that governments on both side of the Atlantic
need to get into their heads.

In the preface to this book I referred to the fact that even
the report by the American 9/11 Commission scarcely mentions al-Qa'ida's ideological bedrock. Instead the report gives
the impression that Islamism first arose in response to current
American and Western policies.

This begins with a remark on the early days of Islamism,
when, we are told, "Fundamentalists helped articulate anticolo-
nial grievances", as if the Muslim Brothers of the 1930s had set
themselves the priority of supporting a historically legitimate
protest movement. The message that the West is guilty is repeated
in the analysis of bin Laden's motives: "Bin Laden's grievances
with the United States may have started in reaction to specific
US policies but it quickly became far deeper." The truth is that
the al-Qa'ida leader was not politicized by "specific US policies",
but by the jihadist lectures of Muhammad Qutb and Abdullah
Azzam. The result is a correspondingly one-sided explanation
of al-Qai'da's successes: "As political, social, and economic problems created flammable societies, Bin Laden used Islam's most
extreme fundamentalist traditions as his match."

353. Tawfik Hamid, 'The Trouble With Islam' *Wall Street Journal*, April 3,
2007.

It is of course true that Islamists seek to exploit real social problems for their own ends. But as a rule Islamism is not the match that bursts into flames of protest as it rubs against real social injustice, but the provider of the explosives with whose help everything that might promote a positive development of the Muslim personality - cinema and theatre, sensuousness and women's equality, scientific inquiry and self-determination - is wantonly destroyed. The radicalisation of Islam is less a consequence of poverty and lack of opportunity than its cause. If we refuse to see this, to recognise the substance of the Islamist ideology - the death cult, antisemitism and hatred of freedom – we will again and again end up "discovering" the sole "root cause" of terrorism in US policies.

Political scientist Andrei S. Markovits has analysed how this process has worked in Europe: "As of October 2001, six to eight weeks after 9/11 and just before the impending American war against the Taliban regime in Afghanistan, a massive Europe-wide resentment of America commenced that reached well beyond American policies, American politics, and the American government and proliferated in virtually all segments of Western Europe's publics. ... For the first time, anti-Americanism has entered the European mainstream."[354]

The refusal to recognize al-Qa'ida's real motives results in a paradoxical reversal of responsibility: the more terrorism, the greater is American guilt. The greater the death toll in America, the stronger anti-Americanism becomes worldwide.

The mass appeal of this effect is related to the hope it holds out: if the frightening phenomenon of suicide terrorism has its roots in US policy, then a change to that policy can take the fear

---

354. Andrei S. Markovits, *Uncouth Nation. Why Europe Dislikes America* (Princeton: Princeton University Press, 2007), p. 3. On the strategic dimension of European policy, which wavers between allying with the USA against Islamism or with Islamism against the USA see: http://www.matthiaskuentzel.de/contents/a-dubious-achievement-joschka-fischer-the-road-map-and-the-gaza-pullout

away. The more alarming the situation, the greater the need for reassurance. Al-Qa'ida can feed off this phenomenon, since the bloodier the attacks in Europe, the greater the anger against... the USA.

We find the same pattern in the bizarre reaction to the Middle East conflict: The average observer, ignorant of the antisemitic content of the Hamas Charter, has to find another explanation for anti-Jewish terrorism, which has to be: Israel!

Thus suicide terrorism, which Westerners find completely incomprehensible, is rationalised as an act of despair. Here too, following the principle of "the more barbaric the anti-Jewish terror, the greater the Israeli guilt", the victims of the attacks become the source and scapegoat for global terrorism. Willingly or not, the old stereotype of the "the Jew is guilty" is thus amplified in contemporary form – a development that only strengthens the terrorist's determination: "The absence of clarity is the beginning of complicity."[355]

It is to be feared that the "blind struggle" against Islamism – by which I mean one which ignores its ideology – will end in the defeat of the West. The attribution of guilt to Israel and the USA adds fuel to the flames of Islamist propaganda and drives the wedge deeper into the Western camp rather than where it belongs – in the Muslim world.

The Islamists do not hide what they are all about. Osama bin Laden's main reproach against the Americans in his *Letter to the American People* is that they talk and act as free citizens who make their own laws instead of accepting *sharia*[356]. The same hatred of freedom and liberalism can also be found in Mahmud Ahmadinejad's letter to the American President of May 2006. As he puts in triumphantly, "Those with insights can already hear

---

355. Omer Bartov, 'He Meant What He Said. Did Hiterism die with Hitler?' *The New Republic*, February 2, 2004, pp. 25-33.
356. see p. 130

the sounds of the shattering and fall of the ideology and thoughts of the liberal democratic systems."

The letter also propagates a toned-down version of the Islamists' frightful slogan – *you love life, we love death.* "An evil end is in store for those who prioritise life in this world. The eternal joy of paradise awaits those who fear the Lord and do not follow their lusts."[357] As we can see, the Islamists do not criticise the Americans primarily because of what they do, but for what they are – a freedom loving and life-oriented civilisation.

But how can the West successfully fight against its foes if it feels obliged to explain terrorism as a result of its own behaviour? The "blind struggle" has a doubly counter-productive effect: it plays into the hands of the Islamists, who want to divide the West, and it stymies any Western offensive for enlightenment and self-determination, which is the only way to split the majority of Muslims from the Islamists. If we do not challenge the ideological roots of Islamism, it will be impossible to confront the Muslim world with the real alternative: will it choose an orientation towards life or towards death? Will it stand up for individual and social self-determination or submit to the programme of uniformity of a death-obsessed clique of Mullahs and its integral Jew-hatred?

357.   The Iranian regime continues to honour tens of thousands of Iranian children who were sent to certain death across minefields during the war against Iraq. See my article, 'Ahmadinejad's Demons', *The New Republic*, April 24, 2006.

BIBLIOGRAPHY

· · · · · · · · · · · · · · · ·

Al-Awaisi, Abd Al-Fattah Muhammad, *The Muslim Brothers and the Palestine Question 1928-1947* (London: Tauris Academic Studies, 1998)

Hasan Al-Banna, To What Do We Summon Mankind?, in: *Five Tracts of Hasan Al-Banna*, Translated from the Arabic and annotated by Charles Wendell, (Berkely: University of California Press, 1978)

"Ziad Abu-Amr, Shaykh Ahmad Yasin and the Origins of Hamas" in R. Scott Appleby (ed.), *Spokesmen for the Despised. Fundamentalist Leaders of the Middle East* (Chicago: University of Chicago Press, 1997)

R. Scott Appleby (ed.), *Spokesmen for the Despised. Fundamentalist Leaders of the Middle East* (Chicago: University of Chicago Press, 1997)

Walter Armbrust (ed.), *Mass Mediations. New Approaches to Popular Culture in the Middle East and Beyond* (San Francisco: The University of California Press, 2000)

Seth Arsenian, "Wartime Propaganda in the Middle East," *Middle East Journal*, Vol. 2, No. 4 (1948)

Ralf Balke, *Die Landesgruppe der NSDAP in Palästina*, thesis, (Universität-Gesamthochschule Essen, 1997)

S. Barel, "Tatsachen zum Nahostkonflikt," in Michael Landmann, *Das Israel-Pseudos der Pseudolinken* (Berlin: Colloquium Verlag, 1971)

Omer Bartov, "He Meant What He Said. Did Hitlerism die with Hitler?," in: *The New Republic*, February 2, 2004

Kirk J. Beattie, *Egypt during the Nasser Years. Ideology, Politics and Civil Society* (New York: Westview Press, 1994)

Joel Beinin, Zachary Lockman, *Workers on the Nile. Nationalism, Communism, Islam and the Egyptian Working Class 1882-1954*, (Princeton NJ: Princeton University Press, 1987

Gal Ben-Ari, *Die Saat des Hasses, Juden und Israel in den arabischen Medien* (Holzgerlingen: Hänssler-Verlag, 2002)

A. Bennigsen, Paul B. Henze, George K. Tanham, S. E. Winbush, *Soviet Strategy and Islam* (London: Palgrave Macmillan, 1989)

Paul Berman, *Terror and Liberalism* (New York: W.W. Norton, 2003)

Reiner Bernstein, *Geschichte des Staates Israel II. Von der Gründung 1948 bis heute* (Schwalbach/Ts.: Wochenschau-Verlag, 1998)

Nicholas Bethell, *The Palestinian Triangle. The struggle between the British, the Jews and the Arabs 1935-48* (London: Andre Deutsch Ltd., 1979)

Yossef Bodansky, *Bin Laden. The Man Who Declared War on America* (Rocklin: Prima Publishing, 1999)

Andrew G. Bostom, ed., *The Legency of Jihad. Islamic Holy War and the Fate of Non-Muslims* (Amherst: Prometheus Books, 2005)

Johan Bouman, *Der Koran und die Juden*, (Darmstadt: Wissenschaftliche Buchgesellschaft, 1990)

Carl Brockelmann, *Geschichte der islamischen Völker und Staaten*, (München und Berlin: R. Oldenbourg, 1939)

Edmond Cao-Van-Hoa, *"Der Feind meines Feindes..." Darstellungen des nationalsozialistischen Deutschland in ägyptischen Schriften* (Frankfurt-am-Main: Peter Lang, 1990)

Hayyim J. Cohen, "The Anti-Jewish Farhud in Baghdad, 1941," *Middle Eastern Studies*, Vol. 3, October 1966, No. 1, pp. 2-17.

Hillel Cohen, *Army of Shadows. Palestinian Collaboration With Zionism 1917-1948*, Forthcoming from University of California Press in 2007.

Michael Cohen, *Retreat from the Mandate* (New York, 1978)

Joseph Croitoru, *Hamas. Der islamische Kampf um Palästina* (Munic : Beck-Verlag 2007)

Deutsche Welle, ed., *Wortschlacht im Äther. Der deutsche Auslandsrundfunk im Zweiten Weltkrieg* (Berlin: Haude & Spenersche Verlagsbuchhandlung, 1971)

Wolfgang Driesch, *Islam, Judentum und Israel*, Deutsches Orient-Institut, Mitteilungen Band 66 (Hamburg, 2003)

Michael Doran, *Pan-Arabism before Nasser* (New York: Oxford University Press, 1999)

Ulrike Dufner, *Islam ist nicht Islam. Die türkische Wohlfahrtspartei und die ägyptische Muslimbruderschaft: Ein Vergleich ihrer politischen Vorstellungen vor dem gesellschaftspolitischen Hintergrund* (Opladen: Leske + Budrich, 1998)

Christian Eggers, 'Die Juden werden brennen' - Die antisemitischen Wahnvorstellungen der Hamburger Al Qaida-Zelle um Mohammed Atta, " in Matthias Küntzel, "Heimliches Einverständnis?" Islamischer Antisemitismus und deutsche Politik (Münster: LIT-Verlag, 2007)

Zvi Elpeleg, *The Grand Mufti. Hajj Amin al-Hussaini, Founder of the Palestinian National Movement* (London: Frank Cass, 1993)

Kurt Fischer-Weth, *Amin al-Husseini. Großmufti von Palästina* (Berlin: Walter Tietz, 1943)

Joel Fishman, "The Big Lie and the Media War Against Israel: From Inversion of the Truth to Inversion of Reality," in: *Jewish Political Studies Review* 19, nos. 1 & 2 (Spring 5767/2007)

Albrecht Fuess, "Propaganda at the Pyramids: The German Community in Egypt 1919-1939," in Wageh Atik, Wolfgang G. Schwanitz (eds.), *Ägypten und Deutschland im 19. und 20. Jahrhundert im Spiegel der Archivalien* (Cairo: Dar ath-Thaqafa, 1998)

Klaus Gensicke, *Der Mufti von Jerusalem Amin el-Husseini und die Nationalsozialisten* (Frankfurt-am-Main: Peter Lang, 1988)

Israel Gershoni, James P. Jankowski, *Redefining the Egyptian Nation 1930-1945* (Cambridge UK: Cambridge University Press, 1995)

Andrew Gowers and Tony Walker, *Arafat, Hinter dem Mythos* (Hamburg: Europäische Verlagsanstalt, 1994)

D.F. Green, ed., *Arab Theologians on Jews and Israel* (Genève: Editions de l'Avenir, 1971)

Fritz Grobba, *Männer und Mächte im Orient* (Göttingen: Musterschmidt, 1967)

Yvonne Haddad, "Islamists and the ‚Problem of Israel': the 1967 Awakening," in *Middle East Journal*, volume 46, no, 2, pp. 278ff.

Michael Hagemeister, "'Die Protokolle der Weisen von Zion' and der Basler Zionistenkongress von 1897," in Heiko Haumann (ed.), *Der Erste Zionistenkongress von 1897 - Ursachen, Bedeutung, Aktualität* (Basle, 1997)

Heiko Haumann (ed.), *Der Erste Zionistenkongress von 1897 - Ursachen, Bedeutung, Aktualität* (Basle, 1997)

Thomas Haury, "Der Antizionismus der Neuen Linken in der BRD," in Arbeitskreis Kritik des deutschen Antisemitismus (ed.), *Antisemitismus - die deutsche Normalität, Geschichte und Wirkungsweise des Vernichtungswahns* (Freiburg: Ça ira, 2001)

Jeffrey Herf, *Divided Memory: The Nazi Past in the Two Germanys* (Harvard University Press, 1997)

Jeffrey Herf, *Reactionary Modernism: Technology, Culture and Politics in Weimar and the Third Reich* (New York: Cambridge University Press, 1984)

Jeffrey Herf, *The Jewish Enemy. Nazi Propaganda during World War II and the Holocaust* (Campbridge MA and London: Harvard University Press 2006)

Jeffrey Herf, ed., *Anti-Semitism and Anti-Zionism in Historical Perspective: Convergence and Divergence* (London: Routledge/ Taylor and Francis, 2006)

J. Heyworth-Dunne, *Religious and Political Trends In Modern Egypt*, published by the author, Washington 1950

Dilip Hiro, *Holy Wars. The Rise of Islamic Fundamentalism* (New York, Routledge, 1989)

Lukasz Hirszowicz, *The Third Reich and the Arab East* (London: Routledge & Kegan Paul, 1966)

Adolf Hitler, *Mein Kampf* (Vol. II – Munich: Verlag Franz Eher Nachfolger, 1925)

Gerhard Höpp (ed.), *Mufti-Papiere. Briefe, Memoranden, Reden und Aufrufe Amin al-Husainis aus dem Exil 1940-1945* (Berlin, Klaus Schwarz, 2001)

J. C. Hurewitz, *The Struggle for Palestine* (New York: Norton, 1951)

James Jankowski, "Egyptian Responses to the Palestine Problem in the Interwar Period," *International Journal of Middle East Studies*, Vol. 12 (1980)

James Jankowski, Israel Gershoni, *Rethinking Nationalism in the Arab Middle East* (New York: Columbia University Press, 1997)

James Jankowski, "Nasserism and Egyptian State Policy 1952-1958," in James Jankowski, Israel Gershoni, *Rethinking Nationalism in the Arab Middle East* (New York: Columbia University Press, 1997)

Johannes J. G. Jansen, *The Dual Nature of Islamic Fundamentalism* (London: Hurst & Company, 1997)

Taysir Jbara, *Palestinian Leader Hajj Amin al-Husayni, Mufti of Jerusalem* (Princeton: Kingston Press, 1985)

Nels Johnson, *Islam and the Politics of Meaning in Palestinian Nationalism* (London: Kegan Paul International, 1982)

Gilles Kepel, *Das Schwarzbuch des Dschihad. Aufstieg und Niedergang des Islamismus* (Munich: Piper, 2002)

David Kimche, *The Last Option. After Nasser, Arafat and Saddam Hussein* (London: Weidenfeld and Nicolson, 1991)

Kisch, Frederick H., *Palestine Diary* (London: Gollancz Ltd.,1938)

Franz Kogelmann, *Die Islamisten Ägyptens in der Regierungszeit von Anwar as-Sadat (1970-1981)* (Berlin: Klaus Schwarz Verlag, 1994)

Gudrun Krämer, *Minderheit, Millet, Nation? Die Juden in Ägypten 1914-1952* (Wiesbaden: Verlag Otto Harrassowitz, 1982)

Gudrun Krämer, *Gottes Staat als Republik. Reflexionen zeitgenössischer Muslime zu Islam. Menschenrechten und Demokratie* (Baden-Baden: Nomos-Verlagsgesellschaft, 1999)

Martin Kramer, "Hizbullah: The Calculus of Jihad", in: Martin E. Marty und R. Scott Appleby, *Fundamentalisms And The State*, (Chicago: University of Chicago Press, 1993)

Matthias Küntzel, Ulrike Becker, Klaus Thörner et al., *Goldhagen und die deutsche Linke* (Berlin, Elefanten Press, 1997)

Matthias Küntzel, *Der Weg in den Krieg. Deutschland, die NATO und das Kosovo* (Berlin: Elefanten Press, 2000)

Matthias Küntzel, "National Socialism and Antisemitism in the Arab World," *Jewish Political Studies Review*, Spring 2005, Vol. 17, No. 1 & 2, pp. 99-118.

Matthias Küntzel, "The Booksellers of Tehran," in: *The Wall Street Journal*, October 28, 2005, p. W 10.

Matthias Küntzel, "Ahmadinejad's Demons," in: *The New Republic*, April 24, 2006, pp. 15-23.

Matthias Küntzel, "From Khomeini to Ahmadinejad," in: *Policy Review*, December 2006 & January 2007, No. 140, pp.69-80.

Matthias Küntzel, "Unholy Hatreds: Holocaust Denial and Antisemitism in Iran", *Posen Paper in Contemporary Antisemitism no. 8*, published by the Vidal Sassoon International Center of the Study of Antisemitism, The Hebrew University of Jerusalem, 2007

Matthias Küntzel, *"Heimliches Einverständnis?" Islamischer Antisemitismus und deutsche Politik* (Münster: LIT-Verlag, 2007)

Uri M. Kupferschmidt, *The Supreme Muslim Council. Islam under the British Mandate for Palestine* (Leiden: E. J. Brill, 1987)

Michael Landmann, *Das Israel-Pseudos der Pseudolinken* (Berlin: Colloquium Verlag, 1971)

Walter Laqueur, *A History of Zionism* (New York: Schocken Books, 1972)

Walter Laqueur, Barry Rubin (eds.) *The Israel-Arab Reader. A Documentary History of the Middle East Conflict* (New York: Penguin Books, 1984)

Walter Laqueur, *The Changing Face of Anti-Semitism: From Ancient Times to the Present Day* (New York: Oxford University Press, 2006)

Brynjar Lia, *The Society of the Muslim Brothers in Egypt* (Reading: Ithaca Press, 1988)

Bernard Lewis, *Semites and Anti-Semites* (London: Weidenfeld and Nicolson, 1986)

Bruse Maddy-Weitzman, *The Crystallization of the Arab State System 1945-1954* (New York: Syracuse University Press, 1993)

Anton Maegerle, "Djihad gegen Juden und Israel," *Tribüne*, Vol. 44, no. 173, p. 185.

Martin E. Marty und R. Scott Appleby, *Fundamentalisms And The State*, (Chicago: University of Chicago Press, 1993)

Klaus-Michael Mallmann/Martin Cüppers, *Halbmond und Hakenkreuz. Das Dritte Reich, die Araber und Palästina* (Darmstadt: Wissenschaftliche Buchgesellschaft, 2006)

Philip Mattar, *The Mufti of Jerusalem. Al-Hajj Amin al-Husayni and the Palestinian National Movement* (New York: Columbia University Press, 1988)

Andrei S. Markovits, *Uncouth Nation. Why Europe Dislikes America* (Princeton: Princeton University Press, 2007)

Thomas Mayer, "Arab Unity of Action and the Palestine Question 1945-48," in: *Middle Eastern Studies*, Vol. 22, No. 3, July 1986, p. 344.

Hermann Meier-Cronemeyer, *Geschichte des Staates Israel, Vol 1* (Schwalbach/Ts.: Wochenschau-Verlag, 1997)

Wilhelm Meister (pseudonym), *Judas Schuldbuch. Eine deutsche Abrechnung* (Munic: Deutscher Volksverlag 1919)

Robert Melka, *The Axis and the Arab Middle East 1930-1945*, (thesis, University of Minnesota, University Micro- films, Inc., Ann Arbor, MI, 1966)

Beverley Milton-Edwards, *Islamic Politics in Palestine* (London: Tauris Academic Studies, 1996)

Naila Minai, *Schwestern unterm Halbmond. Muslimische Frauen zwischen Tradition und Emanzipation* (Munich: Klett-Cotta, 1989

Schaul Mishal and Reuben Aharoni, *Speaking Stones. Communiqués from the Intifada Underground* (Syracuse: Syracuse University Press, 1994)

Richard P. Mitchell, *The Society of the Muslim Brothers* (London: Oxford University Press, 1969)

Adnan Musallam, *Sayyid Qutb, The Emergence of the Islamist 1939-1950* (Jerusalem: Passia Publication, 1997)

Mordechai Naor, *Eretz Israel. Das 20. Jahrhundert* (Cologne: Könemann, 1998)

Laurie Mylroie, *Study of Revenge* (Washington DC: The AEI Press, 2000)

Ronald L. Nettler, *Past Trials and Present Tribulations: A Muslim Fundamentalist's View of the Jews* (Oxford: Pergamon Press, 1987)

Götz Nordbruch, "Holocaustleugnung und Kampf gegen 'Normalisierung'. Arabische Diskussionen um den Holocaust" in *Der Rechte Rand*, nr. 72, Sept/Oct 2001, pp. 19ff.

Götz Nordbruch, *Narrating Palestinian Nationalism. A Study of the New Palestinian Textbooks* (Washington, The Middle East Media Research Institute, 2002)

Léon Poliakov, *Vom Antizionismus zum Antisemitismus* (Freiburg: ca ira, 1992)

Yehuda Porath, *The Palestinian Arab National Movement. From Riots to Rebellion*, Vol. II, 1929-1939 (London: Frank Cass, 1977)

Itamar Rabinovich, "Germany and the Syrian Political Scene in the late 1930s," in Jehuda L. Wallach (ed.), *Germany and the Middle East 1835-1939*, (International Symposium of the University of Tel Aviv: Nateev-Press, April 1975)

Alfred Rosenberg, *Der staatsfeindliche Zionismus*, citations from the 1938 Munich edition (Zentralverlag der NSDAP, Munich, 1938)

Barry Rubin, *Islamic Fundamentalism in Egyptian Politics* (London: Macmillan, 1990)

Josef B. Schechtman, *The Mufti and the Fuehrer* (New York – London: Thomas Yoseloff, 1965)

David Th. Schiller, *Palästinenser zwischen Terrorismus und Diplomatie. Die paramilitärische palästinensische Nationalbewegung won 1918 bis 1981* (Munich: Bernard & Graefe, 1982)

Gerhard Schulz (ed.) *Die Große Krise der dreißiger Jahre. Vom Niedergang der Weltwirtschaft zum Zweiten Weltkrieg* (Göttingen: Vandenhoeck & Ruprecht, 1985)

Wolfgang G. Schwanitz (eds.), *Ägypten und Deutschland im 19. und 20. Jahrhundert im Spiegel der Archivalien* (Cairo: Dar ath-Thaqafa, 1998)

Werner Schwipps, "Wortschlacht im Äther," in Deutsche Welle, ed., *Wortschlacht im Äther. Der deutsche Auslandsrundfunk im Zweiten Weltkrieg* (Berlin: Haude & Spenersche Verlagsbuchhandlung, 1971)

Eberhard Serauky, *Im Namen Allahs. Der Terrorismus im Nahen Osten* (Berlin: Dietz, 2000)

Albert Speer, *Spandauer Tagebücher*, Frankfurt/Main 1975

Fritz Steppat, "Das Jahr 1933 und seine Folgen für die arabischen Länder des Vorderen Orients" in Gerhard Schulz (ed.) *Die Große Krise der dreißiger Jahre. Vom Niedergang der Weltwirtschaft zum Zweiten Weltkrieg* (Göttingen: Vandenhoeck & Ruprecht, 1985)

Ted Swedenburg, "Sa'ida Sultan/Dana International: Transgender Pop and the Polysemiotics of Sex, Nation and Ethnicity on the Israeli-Egyptian Border," in Walter Armbrust (ed.), *Mass Mediations. New Approaches to Popular Culture in the Middle East and Beyond* (San Francisco: The University of California Press, 2000)

The 9/11 Commission Report (New York: Cambridge University Press, 1984)

Bassam Tibi, *Islamischer Fundamentalismus, moderne Wissenschaft und Technologie* (Frankfurt am Main: Suhrkamp, 1992)

Bassam Tibi, *Fundamentalismus in Islam. Eine Gefahr für den Weltfrieden?* (Darmstadt: Wissenschaftliche Buchgesellschaft, 2000a), p. 117;

Bassam Tibi, *Der Islam und Deutschland. Muslime in Deutschland* (Stuttgart: Deutsche Verlags-Anstalt, 2000b)

Bassam Tibi, *Die neue Weltordnung. Westliche Dominanz und islamischer Fundamentalismus* (Munich, 2001a)

Bassam Tibi, *Kreuzzug und Djihad. Der Islam und die Christliche Welt* (Munich: Goldmann, 2001b)

Daphne Trevor, *Under the White Paper* (Jerusalem: Jerusalem Press, 1948)

Lionel van der Meulen, *Fremde im eigenen Land. Die Geschichte der Palästinenser und der PLO* (Munich: Knesebeck & Schuler, 1989)

Janet Wallach, John Wallach, Arafat. *In the Eyes of the Beholder* (New York: Carol Publishing Group, 1990)

Jehuda L. Wallach (ed.), *Germany and the Middle East 1835-1939*, (International Symposium of the University of Tel Aviv: Nateev-Press, April 1975)

Simon Wiesenthal, *Großmufti – Großagent der Achse* (Salzburg-Wien: Ried-Verlag, 1947)

Giselher Wirsing, *Engländer, Juden, Araber in Palästina*, fifth revised edition (Leipzig: Eugen Diederichs Verlag, 1942)

Robert Wistrich, *Hitler's Apocalypse, Jews and the Nazi Legacy*, (London: Weidenfeld & Nicolson, 1985)

Robert Wistrich, *Muslim Antisemitism; a Clear and Present Danger* (American Jewish Committee, Washington 2002)

Bat Ye'or, *Islam and Dhimmitude. Where Civilizations Collide*, (Cranbury, NJ: Associated University Presses, 2002)

Michael Youssef, *Revolt Against Modernity. Muslim Zealots and the West* (Leiden: E.J. Brill, 1985)

INDEX

· · · · · · ·